Teaching the Internet in Libraries

RACHEL SINGER GORDON

AMERICAN LIBRARY ASSOCIATION
Chicago and London
2001

Phillips Memorial Library
DISCARD

025.04
G672T

While extensive effort has gone into ensuring the reliability of information appearing in this book, the publisher makes no warranty, express or implied, on the accuracy or reliability of the information, and does not assume and hereby disclaims any liability to any person for any loss or damage caused by errors or omissions in this publication.

Trademarked names appear in the text of this book. Rather than identify or insert a trademark symbol at the appearance of each name, the author and the American Library Association state that the names are used for editorial purposes exclusively, to the ultimate benefit of the owners of the trademarks. There is absolutely no intention of infringement on the rights of the trade-mark owners.

Project manager: Joan A. Grygel

Cover and text design: Dianne M. Rooney

Composition by ALA Editions in QuarkXpress 4.11 using a Macintosh platform.

Printed on 50-pound white offset, a pH-neutral stock, and bound in 10-point cover stock by McNaughton & Gunn

The paper used in this publication meets the minimum requirements of American National Standard for Information Sciences—Permanence of Paper for Printed Library Materials, ANSI Z39.48-1992. ∞

Library of Congress Cataloging-in-Publication Data

Gordon, Rachel Singer.
 Teaching the Internet in libraries / by Rachel Singer Gordon.
  p.   cm.
 Includes bibliographical references and index.
 ISBN 0-8389-0799-7
  1. Internet searching—Study and teaching—United States. 2. Computer network resources—Study and teaching—United States.   I. Title.
 ZA4201.G64 2001
 025.04′071—dc21   00-052564

Copyright © 2001 by the American Library Association. All rights reserved except those which may be granted by Sections 107 and 108 of the Copyright Revision Act of 1976.

Printed in the United States of America.

05 04 03 02 01   5 4 3 2 1

CONTENTS

INTRODUCTION

Teaching the Internet in Libraries is intended for Internet trainers, technology coordinators, and administrators at libraries that are beginning either to plan out an Internet training program for the public or to expand and reevaluate their existing classes. You will not find advice here on how to plan, pay for, and manage Internet access in your library or on how to formulate an Internet policy for the public. These topics have been addressed at length in a variety of other books and articles on the subject of providing patron Internet access in libraries. What previous discussions have largely neglected, however, are the practical issues stemming from the need for libraries to provide instruction to the public on the use of the Internet and related electronic resources. This book will assume that you either already have public Internet access in place in your institution or that you have plans to provide such access in the near future. The following chapters will help you provide training classes to help your community take full advantage of the availability of open Internet access and of web-based subscription databases in your library. Although the information and examples focus mainly on public libraries, these general principles and ideas can be adapted to help academic, school, and corporate librarians facing similar training challenges in creating their own programs.

Chapter 1 describes the growing importance of libraries as alternative access points for Internet users and details the many reasons for a library to offer public Internet training. Here you will also find a number of arguments to help convince your administration of the need for developing an Internet training program at your institution.

Chapter 2 talks about choosing and training Internet trainers. It outlines the qualities of a successful trainer and provides ideas for planning, paying for training of Internet instructors, and helping libraries prepare their selected trainers to become effective teachers of technology to the public.

Chapter 3 gets to the details of establishing an Internet training program in your library. Here you will find hints for establishing the training environment, including how to select computer hardware and software and how to set up your sessions. This chapter also discusses how to outline your training sessions and create training aids, such as handouts and "cheat sheets," and computer-based presentations. It concludes with a discussion of the usefulness of computer-based training and Internet tutorials.

Chapter 4 shows you how to add variety to your program of instruction by providing training sessions for diverse groups within your community. Specific ideas outlined here are classes for absolute beginners, native Spanish speakers, parents and teachers, and the elderly.

Chapter 5 expands on the topic of creating variety by discussing how to develop Internet classes on specific topics. Those mentioned include Internet job searching, genealogy, web-based e-mail, and evaluation of online information. The chapter concludes with a discussion of teaching electronic information literacy. This can be accomplished in part by providing classes on the use of your library's web-based catalog and other online databases, and showing when the use of each is appropriate.

Chapter 6 provides examples of as well as suggestions on how to adapt for your own library innovative Internet training programs that have been successful in several different library systems. These include ideas for recruiting volunteer trainers from the local community, examples of libraries that have taken Internet training "on the road," and ways to support the library (or the training program itself) through establishing fee-based Internet classes.

Chapter 7 covers evaluation of your program as a whole, of class content, and of specific trainer presentation and training skills. It gives suggestions on using feedback to improve the Internet training experience so that it provides more value to your patrons.

Appendix A lists recommended books, articles, and web sites for developing an Internet training program in your library. It includes resources on computer training and on teaching electronic information literacy in libraries as well as listing more general manuals that will assist librarians in becoming more effective trainers and presenters.

Appendix B provides examples of handouts, sample advertising materials, evaluation forms, and other helpful items for use while planning and teaching class sessions.

Although the particular focus here is on Internet training in libraries, some of the general computer training principles within are also applicable to many other types of public computer classes a library might offer. Your library may want to expand its technology training program beyond basic Internet classes, for example, and provide its patrons with training sessions on topics such as a general introduction to the PC, word processing basics, or the use of graphic software and scanners. It may also wish to offer related classes on the specific use of a web-based OPAC or on subscription databases. (Such classes will be discussed in more detail in chapter 5.)

Because library resources and communities are so varied, no assumptions will be made as to the specific training environment available. Recommendations, examples, and ideas will address all types of libraries and training situations, from teaching a small group of patrons clustered around one terminal to instructing in a fully equipped computer lab with individual workstations and a projection unit attached to the instructor's machine. Most importantly, you will find what other libraries have done and what you can do to enable your patrons to make effective use of Internet resources, both within and outside the library.

A NOTE ON TERMINOLOGY

Most libraries are not creating a full-fledged academic program for their patrons; they are merely providing their community with the opportunity to receive an introduction to the Internet and to learn basic computer skills. The following chapters, therefore, use the terms "class" and "training session" interchangeably to refer to any Internet training sessions provided by libraries. This will hold true whether these classes are forty-five-minute introductions to a group of five patrons standing around one PC or half-day workshops taught to thirty people occupying individual stations in a computer lab. Patrons attending such training sessions will similarly be referred to as "participants," "trainees," "learners," "attendees," and "students," without regard to subtle distinctions among these terms. Trainers will be referred to as "trainers," "instructors," and "teachers," where all of these terms are understood as referring to the types of trainers and training outlined here.

INTERNET ADDRESSES

Suggested Internet sites mentioned throughout were all operational as of spring 2000. Due to the transient nature of the web, however, some may have moved or folded since the publication of this book. If you get a "404: File Not Found" or similar error while accessing one of the addresses listed here, try to back up to the main part of the address before the first single slash mark (/) and see if the particular page has moved to a different location within the same main URL. Addresses provided are only starting points for your own exploration as you begin to plan out your library's program of Internet instruction.

ACKNOWLEDGMENTS

I would like to thank the various participants on the REFORMA and NET-TRAIN e-mail discussion lists who so graciously took the time to share the details of their respective libraries' Internet training programs with me. Thank you also to those librarians who were patient and thorough in responding to my e-mailed queries requesting more detailed information about the programs mentioned on their web pages and to all those who gave permission for their institution's web sites, brochures, and other materials to be reproduced here for the advantage of others. Lastly, thanks to my husband Todd for his patience while I was glued to the computer these many months.

1

Libraries as Alternative Access Points

This book differs from most general computer training manuals you are likely to encounter. Most books and other resources that discuss methods of computer training are aimed at corporate or contract trainers who are teaching the use of a new software package to a company's employees. Most computer training traditionally has been "task-based"—aimed at teaching computer users the steps necessary to carry out the specific duties they will be completing at work each day. Because of this emphasis on job-oriented, task-based learning, librarians teaching Internet classes to the public lack one advantage of their fellow computer trainers. Corporate trainers are generally teaching their students specific job skills, while other independent computer trainers are often instructing their attendees on strategies for passing a particular test. This provides such trainers with largely predetermined basic class content and objectives that will also influence the format and structure of their training sessions. In contrast, the library Internet trainer is usually under a special obligation to create relevance and structure for his or her students. This presents both particular challenges and unique opportunities for libraries.

In many cases, all that visitors to a library's Internet training seminar may want is a basic introduction. They will be interested in getting a look at the Internet, finding out how to get to and move around among different web sites, and seeing ways in which being online can help them in their daily lives. This creates a very different training environment than that of a corporate classroom full of employees being trained in the steps necessary to complete specific, work-related tasks. Beyond including instruction on the basic use of the browser software, the content of public Internet training sessions will often largely be influenced by the interests of the participants. Demonstrating sites and searches in trainees' areas of interest will help them get the "feel" of being online, while some hands-on practice with the browser functions will give them the tools they need to move around on the Internet.

Library Internet trainers will be teaching patrons about the basic use of browser software and demonstrating a variety of web sites. They will be showing their patrons what they can find and do online. Some participants may come to a library's Internet training class because they are interested in finding out how to accomplish a specific goal, such as locating and purchasing plane tickets online, getting an up-to-the-minute stock quote, or setting up an e-mail account. Others may just want to see what the hype is all about.

Due to limited resources and security concerns, when we talk about public Internet use and training in libraries, we are generally talking about the web. Few libraries currently support public access to or provide training on other Internet applications such as Telnet or FTP or on the use of e-mail software such as Microsoft Outlook or Eudora. The ideas and examples in this book, therefore, will generally focus on teaching the use of the web browser software and of specific types of web-based resources in libraries.

Libraries differ from corporations in one other major way. Companies often can justify the expense of Internet and other computer training in terms of their bottom line: Employees need certain skills to carry out their job duties effectively and efficiently. The impact of public Internet training on a library's "bottom line" is somewhat more difficult to measure. A well-designed training program with a formal evaluation system in place, however, will provide you with the statistics and anecdotes necessary to show your library's board and administration the impact of Internet training on your community. (Program and trainer evaluation will be discussed in chapter 7.)

Libraries offering staff and public access to the Internet are, however, similar to corporations in one major aspect. They have learned (or will learn) the same lessons as companies who invested money in computer equipment and software in the expectation that it would instantaneously and automatically enable their employees to work more efficiently. Merely providing access to the Internet and other computer applications is insufficient; people need to be taught how to use technology before it can make a difference in how they do their jobs—or in how they make use of library resources. In many cases, the need to use new technology can slow down the process of completing such previously familiar activities as looking up a book or typing a letter. Libraries providing Internet access without also providing access to training opportunities will be faced with a barrage of requests for on-the-spot assistance from patrons frustrated by the unfamiliar technology.

Libraries experience a demand for Internet training for a variety of reasons. Although some patrons want training to make better use of the library's resources, many institutions are seeing a growing number of patrons seeking Internet and computer training to help them learn to use PCs they have purchased for their home. Many patrons also come to the library to gain experience in using the Internet and other computer technologies, hoping that such experience will help them find a better job or move up within their current workplace.

In this way, libraries providing Internet and other computer training are serving in a somewhat familiar role as literacy centers, except that this time they are teaching technological literacy. Each library must make a decision as to the amount of time and resources it can devote to training patrons on computer and Internet skills beyond that which it spends providing them with those basic competencies they need to use the library effectively.

Libraries with limited resources to expend on training may wish to provide classes only on basic Internet skills or on the use of electronic library resources. They then can refer patrons who request further instruction to appropriate books, videos, and web sites such as ZDNet's Quickstart for new computer owners (http://www.zdnet.com/quickstart). Respect for patrons, though, demands that they be heard and that libraries make some attempt to meet their need for at least some basic instruction on newer technology. Providing Internet instruction is one way for your library to remain relevant in the eyes of its patrons in an era of increasing reliance on computers. It also helps remove the barrier technology can create between patrons and their use of the library; people's biggest reasons for not using libraries' computers is a lack of training on or skills in using technology.

THE INTERNET EXPLOSION IN LIBRARIES

Nearly 95 percent of public libraries currently offer some form of Internet access to their patrons, and the rest will inevitably begin to do so within the next few years.[1] Although the explosion of Internet access and use in public libraries has fostered a host of worries, from concern about the dangers of unfettered access to fear that electronic resources will someday supplant print, most observers will agree that the Internet is here to stay. Surveys consistently show that patrons want their libraries to be involved in offering access to computers and the Internet to those who lack such access at home and that they want librarians to be involved in helping people to locate information online.[2]

A United States National Commission on Libraries and Information Science (NCLIS) study released in April 1998 showed that 44.7 percent of those people accessing the Internet from outside the major locations of home, work, or school used a public library to do so—around 5.6 million individuals.[3] Local public libraries are the first choice, and one of the few free choices, among "alternative access" locations. The number of people using public libraries for Internet access has grown over only the last couple of years as the Internet has become a part of our common vocabulary and as a combination of curiosity and necessity drives more people to seek out such alternative access points. Although the cost of computer ownership and of home Internet access has decreased, the "digital divide" still remains. A large percentage of the population does not have easy access to the Internet from either home or work. Libraries offering public access generally find that demand soon grows to exceed their available supply of terminals.

As the number of people using the Internet in libraries, many for the first time, increases, so too does the need for libraries to provide some sort of guidance and instruction in the use of online resources. The huge increase in online usage at public libraries over the past few years has created an environment in which many patrons interested in the Internet may be newer, or even first-time, computer users. This has created a simultaneous increase in the need for librarians to expand their traditional instructional role into that of computer trainer.

The influx of Internet users also raises the question of how the Internet can most effectively be integrated into the library's traditional mission of connecting its visitors with information and ideas. It is at the very least overly optimistic, and at the worst somewhat obstructive, to expect that library patrons—many of whom may be using a computer, much less the Internet, for the first time—each independently master the art of using and searching the Internet without some form of formal training.

Librarians who have been using the Internet as part of their daily lives for years may easily underestimate how intimidating or confusing it can be for a newer user to sit down in front of a computer. Many of the patrons who need access to online resources will have had little or no experience in using a mouse, interpreting an icon, or sifting out the useful nuggets from the mountains of irrelevant or downright misleading results a seemingly rational online search can produce. Any public Internet training program should be prepared to deal with computer beginners.

As libraries increase the number of resources they offer in a web-based format, from the online catalog to encyclopedias to magazine indexes, a basic familiarity with using the Internet becomes a prerequisite for the effective use of any library. The transformation of libraries' traditional resources into a hybrid of electronic and print formats as well as the explosion of information available online make it imperative that we equip our customers to move into the information age with us.

THE UNIQUE LIBRARY TRAINING ENVIRONMENT

Public library Internet (and other computer) training sessions will differ from those offered in a corporate environment in several important ways beyond that of the basic content of classes. Most corporate employees attending training sessions will have had some previous exposure to computers and generally are just receiving additional training on the use of a new or upgraded software package. Because public libraries and public Internet classes are generally open to all, however, some of your students may never have touched a PC or will have had little or no experience in using a mouse. Therefore, basic computer skills must be presented to these patrons before any specific Internet training can take place. (Strategies for teaching absolute beginners are discussed in chapter 4.) Libraries, too, often lack the resources of some corporations that provide their employees with a training environment that includes well-equipped computer labs and dedicated full-time trainers.

The special nature of public library Internet classes presents other unique challenges. Classes cannot be geared specifically toward attendees' jobs, for example, so each participant may have a different reason for attending. Each will want the class to have a different focus. Many public libraries also lack the resources to either hire a full-time trainer or equip a separate computer lab. Librarians providing Internet training must match their classes to the resources their institutions have available.

Providing Internet training in a library, however, also has unique rewards. One complaint of many corporate computer trainers is that participants often attend their classes only because participation in training sessions is a job requirement. Such employees can feel resentment at having to take time out of their busy schedules to learn a new computer program or system and will show that resentment by expressing hostility toward their trainers or through reluctance to learn the new software. Attendees of library Internet classes, though, generally come to training sessions out of personal interest; they truly want to learn. Library trainers also have the opportunity to reach and teach groups of patrons who otherwise have limited access to computers and training opportunities; therefore, the trainers have the ability to make a real difference in people's lives.

Whether they are showing people how to use an index, conducting a bibliographic instruction seminar, or explaining how to look up materials in a card catalog or OPAC, librarians have always been trainers. The Internet merely presents a new format and set of training challenges. Those who are able to transfer their general training and people skills to the skills needed to teach technology will be at a distinct advantage.

GAINING ADMINISTRATIVE SUPPORT FOR PROGRAMS

In any public library, the library board and director must give their approval for any major initiative such as a new training program. It can sometimes be difficult to convince a library's administration of the importance of establishing or of continuing to fund public Internet classes, especially given the money already spent on bringing technology to the library and on training library staff in the use of a variety of computer applications. Marshal your evidence and arguments carefully to demonstrate the benefits of Internet training to your library and to your community.

If you already have an Internet training program in place, collect evidence of its success and popularity. Save positive evaluation forms, keep statistics on the number of people trained on using the Internet, and elicit anecdotes from your trainers and public services staff. Listen to patrons as they talk to library staff and each other, even if they are complaining about the very presence of computers in the library or about the difficulty of using your web-based catalog. Such complaints can point out a genuine need for instruction on the use of Internet resources. Never assume that the continuation of your Internet training program is assured, and always be ready to demonstrate its value to your board and administrator.

In the best of all possible worlds, your library's administration will be involved with and committed to every step of bringing the Internet to your library, including the establishment of public training sessions. Realistically, however, your board members or director may be somewhat resistant to setting up Internet training for a variety of reasons, ranging from the potential cost of the program to their own fear of newer technology. The following sections will help you convince a recalcitrant administration to focus on the advantages of patron Internet training sessions.

Build on the Predominance of Web-Based Online Catalogs and Databases

If your library's catalog has already moved onto the web, training patrons to use the Internet also effectively helps train them to use the catalog, which will use a familiar web-based interface. This decreases the need for librarians to spend time demonstrating the use of the web-based OPAC and locating materials for people. Internet training will help make patrons more self-sufficient and reduce the unscheduled staff time spent on informal, "walk-up" training of and doing searches for library visitors. Whenever a public services librarian needs to leave the desk and spend time training a patron on the basic use of the OPAC, patrons in need of other types of assistance are left waiting.

If your computer catalog is not yet web-based, chances are it soon will be. Major vendors such as Data Research Associates (DRA), for example, are beginning to phase out support for their older, text-based products. Most computerized library catalogs will eventually use a similar web-based format.

Other electronic databases used in many libraries are also moving away from CD-ROM and text-based products and onto the web, from periodical indexes such as the Gale Group's InfoTrac to reader's advisory resources such as the CARL Corporation's NoveList. Database vendors are now beginning strongly to encourage libraries to use their web-based products, and some are currently or in the near future discontinuing the availability of their offerings in any other format. Print reference sources are moving online as well, and the government's transition to an "electronic depository" system means that many government documents are now or will eventually be accessible only online. The potential cost saving to publishers means that some current print resources will soon be available only on the web.

Furthermore, many state libraries are recognizing the usefulness of electronic information resources and are requesting legislative funding to make selected for-pay Internet databases available in libraries across their states. The Illinois State Library, for example, provides state residents with free access to NoveList and to selected FirstSearch databases through public, school, and academic libraries statewide. If patrons are stymied by the Internet interface to such products, they will be unable to make effective use of the electronic resources provided by their own tax dollars.

Library patrons who are familiar with basic Internet functions and who are comfortable using a mouse, filling in a search form, and using the browser buttons will be able to conduct simple web-based OPAC and database searches with a minimum of instruction. Teaching library patrons how to use the Internet accustoms them to some common interface formats among all of these products, enabling them to make more effective use of the library and reducing some of the pressure to offer large numbers of separate training sessions for each library database. It also allows trainers who are teaching the use of specific electronic resources to focus on those products' particular features during class sessions, rather than taking class time to teach such basics as point-and-click, filling in search forms, and the use of the scroll bars and the browser's back button. Basic Internet skills are now a prerequisite for teaching electronic information literacy.

Train Many People at a Time

Although the need for informal, one-on-one training on a walk-in basis will never entirely be eliminated, formal training sessions can reach large numbers of library users at one time. Offering such classes will reduce the need for librarians to spend time informally training each individual who walks through the door and will allow librarians to present their customers with the option of a scheduled class as an alternative when no staff members are available for on-the-spot training. This reduces the chance that library visitors will leave dissatisfied or frustrated in their attempts to use either the Internet itself or the library's Internet-based OPAC and databases.

Offering training sessions will also help libraries use staff time more efficiently, as extra staff members can be scheduled to cover departments while their colleagues are conducting formal training sessions. Library staff will then be less likely to have to leave a desk unattended or to give short shrift to other patrons while providing often time-consuming individual training on the Internet or on the basic use of the library's electronic resources.

Capitalize on a Publicity Opportunity

Computer classes offered by local community colleges or by technology training institutes can be expensive and are often inaccessible to many of your patrons. Point out to the board and your administrator the public relations bonus that the creation of free or low-cost Internet training classes will offer your institution. Any administration that has gone through a referendum process or fought against tax caps will appreciate the opportunity to keep your library in the public eye by offering high-profile services to the community.

Your library board knows that the Internet is a hot issue and that it will probably remain so for some years to come. Exploit that issue! Adding the title of "Internet trainer" can help improve the public's perceptions of librarians and of the library itself. You want your institution to be seen as a technology leader. When your community gets access to value-added and timely services such as Internet instruction, it will be more likely to fund the library in the future.

The library public wants Internet training opportunities. Many libraries that began offering public Internet access without simultaneously offering training sessions have been surprised by public demand and pressured into throwing together classes at a later date. The Carrollton Public Library (Texas), for example, went online in mid-1996, and at that time it offered its patrons the opportunity to take a training class taught by an outside consultant. The availability of public Internet access created a wave of demand for additional classes, but, due to budget constraints, no more were taught until early 1998—at the point where constant patron requests pressured the library's public services staff into creating and teaching training sessions themselves.

If you are just beginning to offer Internet access in your library, to make the switch from text-only access to the use of graphical web browsers, or to expand your public workstations, plan your training program at the same time and provide your community with a service it will surely be requesting. Listening to your community's needs will help your patrons develop positive feelings toward an institution that invests in their learning.

You want your library to take its place as a technology leader within your community. Present Internet training classes as one of the many technological benefits the library can offer its constituents, and take the opportunity to involve your mayor or other local leaders. Give them some credit for your institution's ability to provide such benefits, making them partners in your library's technology training efforts.

Reduce the Fear of the Internet in Libraries

When it comes to Internet issues, libraries have not generally received the best publicity. Offering classes and showing patrons the wealth of information available online is one of the best ways to reduce the fear of the Internet, which is often really the fear of the unknown. The more familiar your patrons are with the Internet, the less likely they will be to see its presence in the library as a potential or unnecessary evil.

Parents of school-age children are particularly likely to be fearful of the dangers of Internet access—which is hardly surprising, given the inflammatory tone of many articles in the popular press. Classes present an opportunity for you to counteract such anti-Internet messages with your own, positive presentation. Point out to your library board the potential impact of providing public classes geared specifically toward parents. (This is discussed in greater depth in chapter 4.) In such classes, you can show parents the opportunities the Internet offers their children for homework help and learning and the chance it offers them to find parenting information and to communicate with other parents, friends, or relatives online. You will also be able to take the opportunity during training sessions to explain your institution's particular Internet policy and its strategies for guiding children to helpful and appropriate online resources.

Enable Better Public Use of the Library's Web Page

Does your library have a web page? Are your patrons able to make effective use of its resources? Tell your administration about the public relations and outreach opportunities that stem naturally from more people being able to take advantage of your library's presence on the web. Also, the more people who are able to make use of your web page, the greater payback your library receives on the resources it expended in the creation of its site—whether the web design was done in-house or outsourced to another agency.

Demonstrating your web page and its resources during training classes can also help increase the exposure of your library's other programs and services. If your library does not yet have its own web page, it might consider creating even a simple in-house site to support its training classes. Such a web site can be mounted on the library's local network or even on the hard drive of the computer(s) that will be used for instruction. Web space is becoming very affordable, and even librarians with little or no experience in web page construction can create a simple site using software such as Microsoft FrontPage.

Attract a New Group of Patrons

Library use is historically lower among lower income and minority groups, who are also among those least likely to have computers at home. Why not use the availability of Internet classes to draw in groups that are historically underserved and take the opportunity to let them know about the library's other programs? People without computer access at home or work are likely to use the Internet in a public place such as a library, but their previous lack of exposure to the Internet means that these groups are also more likely to need and attend introductory training sessions.

Specific ideas for planning classes for Spanish speaking patrons are outlined in chapter 4, but you can extend that example to plan programs as appropriate for your particular community. Present options for teaching training sessions to different groups, and outline the benefits of such classes to your administration.

Produce Big Results at a Low Cost

Public library boards and administrators often assume that Internet and other computer training sessions will be prohibitively costly for their institution. If your administration is concerned about the potential cost of setting up a training program, present a plan for creating basic classes using existing, or minimal additional, resources. (Affordable options for presenting Internet classes using existing staff and equipment are outlined in chapter 3.)

Although most computer training manuals assume that you will have a teaching lab and the staff to provide full- or half-day sessions, do not let those preconceptions discourage you from creating a training program on a smaller scale. If you have the staff or equipment to provide only a forty-five-minute introductory course to small groups of students clustered around one public terminal, then plan your sessions that way. Your patrons will appreciate that their library is making the effort to provide Internet training, and any exposure to and explanation of Internet resources and software will help provide them with the background for further online exploration on their own.

In presenting whatever arguments are necessary to convince your administration to back Internet training classes, look upon the experience as practice for the future Internet discussions you will probably be involved in on behalf of your institution. Become an advocate for the Internet's ability to make a difference in the lives of your patrons, no matter who your audience.

NOTES

1. U.S. National Commission on Libraries and Information Science, *Public Libraries and the Internet 2000: Summary Findings and Data Tables* (Washington, D.C.: The Commission, 2000). Available: http://www.nclis.gov/statsurv/2000plo.pdf.

2. See, for example, *Buildings, Books, and Bytes: Libraries and Communities in the Digital Age* (Washington, D.C.: The Benton Foundation, 1996). Available: http://www.benton.org/Library/Kellogg/buildings.html.

3. U.S. National Commission on Libraries and Information Science (NCLIS), *Moving toward More Effective Public Internet Access: The 1998 National Survey of Public Library Outlet Internet Connectivity* (Washington, D.C.: US NCLIS, 1999). Available: http://www.nclis.gov/what/1998plo.pdf.

2 Choosing and Training Your Trainers

Just as no one is born knowing how to navigate the Internet, few of us are born knowing how to train others. Your trainers will assimilate technology teaching skills in several ways. The best way to learn, of course, is by doing, and as your Internet trainers gain teaching experience they will also gain confidence in their own skills and increase their ability to communicate computer concepts to others. Your beginning trainers, however, may benefit from some initial train-the-trainer sessions and from learning and practicing presentation techniques before attempting to teach public Internet training sessions themselves.

Luckily for libraries, most librarians are used to acting as trainers either formally or informally in their day-to-day contact with patrons. Many need only to adapt their skills to technology training as the role of Internet trainer becomes natural for librarians. You can help your chosen trainers to enhance their skills by giving them the opportunity and funding to attend training classes. Train-the-trainer sessions will help your trainers assimilate basic technology-training principles, whether such classes are provided at your library, by your library system/consortium, or by an outside training institute or consultant. Also, provide your trainers with easy access to books, videos, and web sites on effective presentation and training techniques, and allow them the opportunity to practice their teaching skills on other staff members.

While computer technology and, thus, the specific content of public classes will change over time, your library's trainers still need to assimilate the basic teaching and presentation skills that will provide the foundation for any effective technology training. They can then go on to develop those skills by training others. Trainers also can help keep their knowledge and skills up to date by attending refresher classes and by independently keeping themselves current, reading up on and practicing with newer technology.

The following sections outline ideas for selecting Internet trainers and for planning and paying for both general staff and trainer training. The process of selecting a trainer will vary from library to library, depending on whether you are hiring a full-time technology trainer or choosing an existing staff member to train in technology and training techniques. Yet all trainers will need to possess similar personal qualities and, preferably, to receive some sort of training themselves before beginning to train others.

CHOOSING TRAINERS

The first step in creating any successful Internet training program is to choose the staff members or outside agents who will serve as instructors. Although the temptation may be to assign responsibility for all computer training to the most technologically skilled member(s) of a library's staff (whether this be a formal information systems department or simply someone with a high comfort level with technology), this is not always the optimal solution. It is a natural assumption to think that the most Internet-savvy staff should make the best trainers, but individuals who are skilled with computers sometimes lack the patience and the people and teaching skills necessary for effective training of computer and Internet beginners.

The Competence Paradox

While technological skills can be learned, skills working with the public and the personality needed to make an effective trainer are not so easily assimilated. Furthermore, computer experts sometimes have a tendency to make assumptions about the knowledge and comfort level of a student. The communication process then breaks down; the computer trainer fails to allow space for questions and experimentation; and it is easy for a student to leave a training session more bewildered than when he or she went in. It is all too common for an expert to forget what it's like to be a beginner.

How often have you seen a computer expert solve a user's problem by taking over the mouse and keyboard and then clicking rapidly through menu options with no explanation of the process involved? Those who are the most comfortable with technology often reach a point where they begin automatically to assume a similar comfort level in others. Such expert users even become unable to recall the specific series of steps it takes to complete a given computer-related task. They have to make a conscious effort to explain the step-by-step process.

These experts have reached a level of "unconscious competence" in their computer skills, where they are able to perform complex tasks without consciously thinking about the process involved.[1] They are likely to lose the vocabulary necessary for breaking down those tasks for users who are less technologically adept.

Elaine Weiss's book *The Accidental Trainer* outlines four levels of competence that learners pass through in the process of mastering any new skill. (See figure 2.1.) Trainers should keep in mind that participants in introductory public Internet classes will most likely be at one of the first two competence levels. Note that the term "incompetent" is not meant here to be

FIGURE 2.1   Levels of Competence

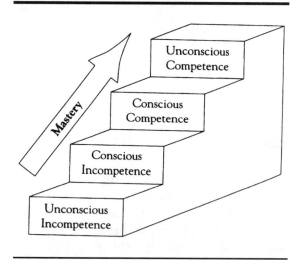

From Elaine Weiss, *The Accidental Trainer: You Know Computers, So They Want You to Teach Everyone Else* (San Francisco: Jossey-Bass Inc., 1997). Reprinted by permission of Jossey-Bass, Inc., a subsidiary of John Wiley & Sons, Inc.

derogatory but is merely used to indicate that a person has not yet mastered a given task.

Individuals at a level of *unconscious incompetence* not only are unable to perform a given skill but they are even unaware that the skill exists. This applies to beginning Internet students who have never seen a computer or touched a mouse and who have never watched another person point the mouse cursor at an icon on the screen and double click to open a program. You will see people at this level of competence walk over to a terminal and pick up the mouse, turn it over and examine it, and possibly even point it at the screen like a remote control.

At the level of *conscious incompetence,* people still aren't able to perform the skill, but they are aware of its existence. If computer beginners have seen another use the mouse to click an icon on the computer screen and open a program, they now know that the mouse is used to point, click, and open programs, but they are unable themselves to use the mouse to do so. They may not know quite where to press to click, they will press both buttons at once, or they will not be sure where on the screen to aim the cursor to open a particular piece of software.

Understanding the last two competence levels is important in assessing potential trainers. People who have just recently learned a skill have reached a level of *conscious competence* in that they can carry out a task but need to consciously remind themselves of each step involved in that task before proceeding. Those at this level will stand at a terminal and think, "All right, now I need to move the cursor here." They will look at the mouse and think about which button to click and how quickly they need to press it.

Finally, those who have mastered the skill (your computer or Internet experts) are at a level of *unconscious competence*—they automatically carry out all of the steps involved in a given task without thinking about them. Individuals at this level will even have difficulty recalling the distinct steps needed to complete a task. When asked to open a program, they will point, double click, and have it open without consciously thinking about how they got to that particular point. This creates the "competence paradox," in which those who have completely mastered a skill are often not the best trainers of others because they have reached a point where it is difficult for them to explain the specific steps involved. Knowing how to use technology does not automatically translate into knowing how to teach it.

Keep these levels of competence in mind when selecting trainers and in training others. In some cases, it will be more effective to provide "consciously competent" librarians with the technology skills necessary to teach the Internet than it will be to try to instill teaching skills in your local computer expert. If you yourself are an expert, or if you are teaching a group of technically skilled library staff members to train the public, remember to emphasize the necessity to break down processes into simple steps. Remember, and remind your trainers, what computing life was like before you were able to move through the system with ease. Trainers need to establish a comfortable balance between technical and training skills.

Qualities of Successful Trainers

Why will librarians in your institution want to become public Internet trainers? After all, creating and teaching training sessions will require extra work and may not be what they envisioned when they went into the field. But it is precisely what we don't envision that keeps us from becoming stagnant in our positions. Giving public service or other librarians the opportunity to train not only helps them to develop their own skills—with the public, with technology, with public speaking, and as a leader—but also helps benefit both the library and your patrons. In general, successful Internet trainers are

> level-headed
>
> comfortable with technology
>
> enthusiastic
>
> patient
>
> comfortable with people

They need to possess a number of personal qualities. High among these is the ability to keep their cool. What will they do if the Internet connection goes down in the middle of a class? How will they handle it if a participant accidentally clicks on a link to a pornography site in the middle of a routine Internet search? Will they be able to respond effectively when they are asked a question that is not strictly pertinent to the class or one to which they may not know the answer? You can help avoid and plan for troublesome situations during public classes with a bit of contingency planning (which will be discussed in the next chapter). None of us, however, has a crystal ball that can help us predict every eventuality. Internet trainers cannot allow themselves to be flustered by unforeseen situations but must be able to continue with the class and even to use such situations as a teaching tool.

In addition to being comfortable dealing with the unforeseen circumstances that go hand-in-hand with both computers and training, an ideal Internet trainer should be comfortable with computer technology. This does not mean that they need to be a "techie." Their technological and people skills need to be balanced, and any public trainers need to be comfortable interacting with others, answering questions, and explaining technical concepts in clear and simple language. Trainers do need to be knowledgeable about computers and the Internet, but they also need to excise computer jargon from their vocabulary when dealing with a class full of beginners.

While keeping their explanations at a level understandable by their students, public Internet trainers also need to be able to communicate their enthusiasm for the subject. It is not necessary that they see the Internet as the pinnacle of human achievement, but they should be excited about its potential and ready to pass that excitement on to others. This enthusiasm should extend to a trainer's desire to keep up his or her own learning about technology because software and sites will be constantly changing. Trainers are always learners.

Use common sense when selecting trainers, and avoid picking librarians who have expressed resentment at the presence and cost of computers or the Internet in libraries or who have qualms about your own library's Internet policy. You want your trainers to promote both the use of the Internet in your institution and your library's Internet policies and programs. Smaller libraries that are adding training to the duties of staff (rather than hiring a trainer whose main duty is to teach) should be careful to choose trainers who will be excited about taking on this role in addition to their other duties rather than being stressed by the idea of assuming an extra responsibility. They should optimally enjoy training and interacting with the public.

Like all computer trainers, Internet instructors need to temper their enthusiasm with patience, taking time to explain the basics without getting ahead of their class. They need to allow learners to proceed at their own pace. Truly patient trainers will be able to empathize with their students and will remember how counterintuitive the use of computers and the Internet seemed when they themselves were just starting out. Patient trainers are developing training skills in all areas. They will listen to questions and clear up confusion and let learners progress naturally rather than jumping ahead or taking over and completing tasks for them.

Trainers are able to resist the temptation to jump directly to their favorite new and cool Internet sites and will summon up the same energy for explaining the use of the browser buttons and other basic topics. Computer experts need to allow beginners the space to experiment and to experience for themselves the process of successfully accomplishing the tasks that have been set as class objectives.

School your library's trainers in the patience needed to avoid taking over the newer user's keyboard or mouse. Show them how to talk people through the steps necessary to complete their objective. Remember that beginners may be uncertain with and even fearful of computer technology and will easily relinquish control to an "expert." However, if an expert solves each problem without allowing students to complete the tasks on their own, the students will never learn the necessary skills to use the Internet independently. Trainers who "do for" their trainees are taking away an opportunity for their students to learn. Such trainers also run the risk of making participants feel slow and inadequate.

Last, trainers should enjoy dealing with the public. Often, libraries automatically choose technical or computer services staff to teach patrons, basing the decision on technical expertise alone. Public services staff often make better Internet trainers (with some technology training of their own) because they are used to dealing with the public on a daily basis. They also may have a better idea of what library Internet users want and are searching for. Select trainers who will be comfortable speaking before a group and who will enjoy the opportunity for interaction with class participants. If you are hiring a new person to be a computer trainer or to provide training as part of his or her official responsibilities, make sure to observe his or her teaching skills prior to making an employment decision. If you have already been selected or volunteered as an Internet trainer or if you are the only one at your library able or willing to teach, keep the previous list of qualities in mind. Examine your own abilities and teaching style to see where you can improve in these areas. People and training skills will be useful in a variety of situations, not just during formal Internet training classes.

Basic Staff and Training Skills

In any library today, all public services staff, especially reference personnel, are in some sense computer trainers. On any given day, any of your library's public services staff members may be called upon to show someone how to accomplish computer-related tasks. These tasks may range from looking up a book in the online catalog to saving a file in a word processing program to signing up for a free web-based e-mail service. Librarians are continually required to provide patrons with informal, on-the-spot training on a variety of computer resources and Internet skills.

Although only one or two library staff members may serve as official Internet trainers, all staff that deal with the public need a solid foundation in basic computer and Internet skills and some ability to transmit such skills to library visitors. It will be helpful to establish a list of core Internet competencies for public services staff and to build upon those requirements for those who will be serving as formal trainers.

Core Internet competencies for all public services staff may include skills such as the following:

> understanding Internet addressing and how to type in a URL to access a particular site
>
> knowing how to use each button on the Netscape or Internet Explorer toolbar
>
> being able to do a keyword search using several major search engines
>
> showing familiarity with the use of an institution's Internet-based subscription resources
>
> using and maintaining bookmarks or favorites
>
> using web-based e-mail, file attachments, and copy/paste
>
> knowing how to download files and print pages from the Internet
>
> understanding how to do an internal keyword search on a long document
>
> doing basic troubleshooting

Place the teaching of these or of similar competencies at the center of general staff Internet training. Mastering such competencies will not only help public services staff teach such skills to patrons but will also help staff carry out their reference duties more effectively. Also, remember that basic computer literacy is a prerequisite for effective Internet use. You may wish to develop a comparable list of core computer competencies that staff should master before moving on to Internet skills, as well as a list of competencies for each specific software program that is heavily used in your library.

Self-assessment forms will help you gauge the skill levels of library staff and the extent to which classes will be necessary. While you can't usually use such assessment tools to help plan patron classes (you want to make patron attendance as easy as possible), staff members can be required to complete such forms prior to their training sessions. Design self-assessment tests to measure the core competencies you have decided on for both general staff and potential public trainers. Keep these simple—ask respondents, for instance, to determine their own competence level on a scale of one to five on a variety of tasks and then total the results for each set of competencies. Determine ranges for the results, and identify where staff are confused on specific programs. Or have staff note whether they are confident, somewhat confident, or not at all confident on each skill, and use those tests to make a note of where training should be focused.

Before training begins, have staff members complete these self-assessment surveys on their own level of computer and Internet savvy. Forms or some other kind of assessment are important because people may under- or overestimate their own technology skills. Often they will essentially be unaware of what they do or do not know about a program. If staff members are comfortable with using online forms, you can post an assessment survey on a web page or on your library's Intranet. An example of an online self-assessment form from the Utah Technology Awareness Project can be seen at http://wwwj1.uen.org/UTAP. Otherwise, traditional paper forms never go out of style. (See appendix B for an example of a staff self-assessment worksheet evaluating Netscape Communicator skills.)

Use the assessments to divide staff and trainers into separate classes based on their skill levels and to identify areas in which skills are weakest. In a smaller library, you may want to provide staff members with individual instruction or send them to separate classes based on their levels of expertise.

Since librarians are almost all now at some point required to act as "trainers," library administrators may also consider making a short demonstration of teaching skills part of the interview process for all public services staff.

Skills of Successful Trainers

Core Internet competencies for full-time or "official" trainers can build upon the previous list of competencies for general public services personnel with the addition of skills that will help the trainers teach classes and field questions from their students. A library may add such requirements as

familiarity with the general history of the Internet

ability to provide a basic definition of the Internet and to explain how it differs from services such as America Online

understanding of the difference between the browser and the Internet and an ISP

ability to explain Internet terminology in simple and clear language

basic knowledge of the use of the operating system and other common software, including the software used in presentations and in creating class handouts

more-advanced troubleshooting skills than those required of other staff

Trainers need to master lists of these or similar competencies while also learning presentation and planning skills.

In a larger system, if possible, designate one person who will be dedicated to coordinating training across your system or consortium. Keeping up with technology is difficult enough for a dedicated trainer, let alone for a busy library professional with a host of other duties. Designating one training coordinator to keep all of your trainers up-to-date on changing technology and training tips will reduce some of the pressure on individual librarians who have training as only one part of their responsibilities.

STAFF TECHNOLOGY TRAINING

Since all public services staff will at some point be called upon to train others, formally or informally, you should preferably provide some sort of computer and Internet training for every staff member. Training sessions can in part be used to impart the kind of core competencies outlined in the previous section for both all public services staff and your Internet trainers.

The next few sections will outline different options for providing and paying for general staff Internet training and for train-the-trainer sessions. A combination of these ideas may be appropriate for your institution.

Using Grant Money

Since computer technology, and especially the Internet, is currently such a hot issue in libraries, grant money for technology training and computer equipment can be somewhat more readily available than it is for other areas. Public libraries have used grants not only for purchasing computer equipment and software but for paying for training sessions for both staff and patrons on a variety of computer and Internet applications.

Using grant money for staff training enhances the services a library is able to offer its community because when staff are up-to-date, they are able to pass that knowledge on to their library users and to use their skills to help locate information for patrons. When researching grants, keep in mind that for training purposes, technology grants, staff development, "bring in an expert," and public services grants may be applicable. Some resources for locating appropriate grants are given later in this section as well as in chapter 6.

Following is an example of how one library used a grant to establish Internet classes for its patrons.

● ●

Librarians at the Addison (Illinois) Public Library (APL) offer a variety of Internet training classes to members of their community, including an introduction to the browser, using search engines, and a basic "Is the Internet for Me?" seminar. These ninety-minute sessions combine demonstrations with hands-on practice in a portable, eight-laptop computer lab that can quickly be set up in the library's meeting room.

In 1998, APL used a Library Services and Technology Act (LSTA) grant from the Illinois State Library to provide a variety of technology training opportunities and resources for its staff, aimed largely at helping them become better trainers of the public.[2] The library used the LSTA grant money to pay for programs and services including

offering staff training by fellow staff members on software programs from Windows 95 to Netscape Communicator 4.5

providing on-site staff training by outside contractors on topics from basic Microsoft Word to PC troubleshooting

sending staff to outside training on more advanced subjects such as Microsoft Visual Basic, FrontPage, and Windows NT administration

purchasing a large screen (35") projection monitor for use in in-house staff and public training sessions

establishing a staff training library of print, video, and CD-ROM resources covering various software titles

purchasing a laptop that staff can borrow and take home for self-study purposes

These training opportunities and additional equipment have enabled APL to offer both better customer service and improved computer training for its patrons, including Internet training.

Expanding on the principle that all public services staff are now "trainers," all members of the information services staff at APL are now required to do some type of computer training, ranging from an introduction to Windows 98 to basic Internet use to using scanning and graphic software. The grant money APL received provided the initial equipment and training that allowed the library to expand its class offerings.

● ●

Many libraries have been able to use grant money for staff and patron Internet training. Gates Library Initiative grants, for example, not only provide money for computer equipment and software but can also provide for training of library staff and supply training materials that library trainers can use when teaching the use of the Internet to their patrons. LSTA grants are another possibility, as are more localized grants from state libraries and associations.

Libraries that are reluctant to apply for grant money for technology and training point to the rapid change inherent in the computer field. They assume that, after the one-time grant period, technology skills and equipment soon will become outdated and are therefore hesitant to put effort into applying for such grants. Using grant money for technology training, however, provides a solid foundation for librarians who will then be more able to develop their individual skills and pass them on to other librarians and the public. Using grant money for equipment, as in establishing a computer lab, allows many more people to be trained at one time. The computer equipment in the lab can then be updated as needed and as funds allow, piece-by-piece, once the initial framework is in place.

When grant money is used to initiate a program, it may then be easier to locate funds for that program's continuation than it would for an entirely new initiative. Furthermore, the use of grant money for essential staff computer training frees up the library's own resources, which can then be spent in other areas.

Locate relevant grant opportunities by checking with your state library and association as well as with ALA and other national library organizations. Keep up with system newsletters, state library journals, and other publications that often list local grant opportunities that may be appropriate for your library. Local grant opportunities are often posted on the web pages of state libraries or associations, while information on and guidelines for the Gates states that are currently eligible for it, can be found online at http://www.gatesfoundation.org/learning/libraries/libraryprogram/usguidelines.htm. A list of ALA grants and a printable application for each is available at http://www.ala.org/work/awards/grants.html. (See chapter 6 for further discussion of using grant money for a library's technology training efforts.)

If your library is ineligible or is turned down for a grant, consider low-cost training options such as using more-experienced staff members to train other staff or attending free or inexpensive seminars offered by local library systems. Also look to community partnerships—would your local chamber of commerce, for example, be willing to donate some money for equipment or staff training in exchange for some publicity and the opportunity for members to attend business-oriented Internet classes later? Libraries have always been creative in funding needed programs, and finding the money to pay for technology training will enable your staff and trainers to pass their skills along to countless others.

Using Staff Members to Train Other Staff

Generally, the most cost-effective staff-training option is to use staff members to train other staff. Training by peers can also increase the comfort level of less technologically skilled participants in your general staff-training sessions. They may feel more comfortable asking questions when the trainer is a fellow employee, and the use of library staff members to train each other provides a level of built-in "technical support" when questions arise after a training session.

Staff members may also be willing to offer one-on-one instruction; this type of training could be prohibitively costly if your library uses a professional trainer to teach sessions. Furthermore, the staff member you choose will be more familiar than any outsider with the library's specific Internet policies and environment. A staff member will already know, for example, which menu options will be blocked by your security software.

Someone on staff should also be tapped to train new employees who may have missed any one-time formal training sessions your institution provided outside the library or given by outside trainers. Training will be an ongoing process as new staff members arrive and as the Internet environment keeps changing.

Paradoxically, using staff to train fellow employees may be most appropriate both in the largest and in the smallest libraries. Using staff may be most viable in larger library districts or systems, which are sometimes able to hire a full-time person devoted to training librarians and to coordinating Internet and other technology training programs systemwide. Using staff to train will be the most affordable option, however, for smaller libraries who are fortunate enough to have a qualified trainer on staff—or at least someone who is willing to learn and to pass on his or her knowledge to others.

Using Outside Agencies/Contractors

If your library lacks the staff to train everyone, or if there is no staff member sufficiently skilled with the Internet or comfortable as a trainer to lead the sessions, then it is time to turn to an outside agency or consultant. Outside trainers are often able to provide a level of expertise that library staff may not possess because these specialists can devote themselves full-time to understanding the intricacies of the Internet; in contrast, librarians have had to add Internet competence to their full plate of existing responsibilities. Furthermore, librarians may accord an outside agent more respect than they would one of their own staff members, recognizing him or her as an expert in the field.

One way to make outside training cost effective is to employ an outside trainer to teach only those librarians who will be responsible for public training sessions and then to have those librarians train other staff members. Using outside trainers may be necessary for at least your train-the-trainer sessions. Although it may not be affordable or practical to provide outside training to all staff members, you need to ensure that those who are "left behind" are brought up to date by those who are able to attend.

Two options in using an outside agency for staff training are bringing trainers to your library or sending staff members to outside classes. Outside classes offer the advantage of being able to train more staff members at once, and such classes also may be taken more seriously. Many of your staff, though, may not be able to attend sessions at the same time—someone has to stay behind and watch the desk. (Check to see if your library system or consortium offers train-the-trainer or Internet-training workshops on a regular basis. Make sure that all appropriate staff members have the opportunity to attend at some point.)

Bringing trainers to your library provides the comfort of familiar surroundings and training on the same equipment and software that librarians will later use to train others. Librarians may learn and retain information more easily when working on familiar equipment, and many libraries use an in-service day once a year to concentrate on staff technology training.

The best way to locate good and affordable outside computer trainers is by asking other libraries in your area about their experiences or by consulting with your library system. You want to choose trainers who are sensitive to the unique library environment. Many former librarians, for instance, have struck out on their own as independent trainers and consultants, and using someone familiar with the library field to conduct staff-training sessions will be beneficial in several ways.

Your library's staff may be more at ease learning training and technology skills from someone who speaks their language and is used to the library environment. Former librarians will also be familiar with the unique challenges presented by public Internet access and training in a library, unlike corporate trainers, who may be used to a very different atmosphere. Librarian/trainers tend to be active contributors to training and library-related e-mail discussion lists, so consider putting out a request on one of those lists for recommendations of trainers in your area. Also, you may be able to tap presenters at local conferences or at events sponsored by large local library systems and organizations to see if those speakers on Internet subjects also provide technology training for librarians.

Consider hiring a consultant through your consortium or system to provide one large-group training session for the trainers at each library. This will spread the cost among several institutions. Consultants generally do most of their work with larger systems and organizations and will be accustomed to tailoring their training to meet the needs of libraries in a particular area.

Examine an outside trainer's promotional material and credentials carefully. Ask for references from other libraries or library systems the trainer has worked with, and follow up on those. Ask if the trainer has a web page you can peruse, and compare the web site of your potential trainer with those of librarian/trainer professionals such as Marylaine Block (http://www.marylaine.com) and Michael Sauers (http://www.bcr.org/~msauers). Does the material look professional? Are the trainer's objectives in line with those you wish to impart to your own trainers? Is the trainer willing to incorporate your objectives and competencies into the training sessions? Technology trainers of librarians should possess the same personal qualities and skills that you desire in your public trainers.

Last, see what training opportunities may be available from your state library or from related institutions. California's InFoPeople Project, for example, is a partnership among the California State Library, the University of California Berkeley Library, and participating local jurisdictions. InFoPeople provides a wide variety of low-cost train-the-trainer sessions and general Internet workshops, from a basic "Teaching the Public to Use the Internet" workshop to classes on teaching the Internet to seniors and using PowerPoint to create presentations. These sessions are open to any information professional in the state. For current course descriptions, see http://www.infopeople.org/workshops/index.html.

TECHNOLOGY TRAINING FOR VOLUNTEERS

Libraries providing Internet and other computer training often find themselves turning to outside volunteers, either to conduct the entire public training program or to fill in the gaps where a particular library lacks personnel or expertise. This can be a cost-effective option for smaller libraries or even for large library systems whose very population creates a heavy demand for public classes. The use of volunteers also frees up librarians and other staff members to concentrate on other tasks. (Examples of libraries with successful and long-running volunteer training programs as well as detailed advice on creating such a program can be found in chapter 6.)

Libraries using volunteers, however, need to invest some time and effort into training those volunteers before allowing them to teach the public. Volunteers will be representing your library, so you want them to be trained to teach the use of the Internet as effectively as one of your own staff members would teach it.

Have potential volunteers observe at least one public training session at your library so that they can see the type of presentation you are looking for and objectives you wish to be covered. Provide them with teaching materials, and especially if you run a larger program, establish some training sessions that will cover the same competencies and principles as any train-the-trainer class for librarians.

AN EFFECTIVE TRAIN-THE-TRAINER PROGRAM

Whether training sessions for public Internet trainers are conducted by outside experts or by other staff members, certain elements should be included. Potential trainers should leave these classes understanding several basic points necessary in effectively training others to use technology.

First, trainers should be able to determine appropriate objectives (or outcomes) for their public Internet classes. Train-the-trainer sessions should go through the process for creating these objectives and for matching class material to the stated objectives. If you are training others to become Internet trainers, stress the need for their class objectives to be clear, realistic, and specific. A realistic objective for a basic Internet class, for example, might be that the participants will leave being able to visit a web site by typing in a URL that they have seen in a commercial, read in an article, or been given by a friend. The number and difficulty of the objectives for a single class will depend on the length of time available and the skill levels of the trainers' students. Objectives are able to be seen or measured; a trainer can observe, for example, whether a student is able to type in a web address to visit a particular site.

Trainers will not be able to transform Internet beginners into Internet experts in one or two class sessions. It is essential that your trainers be able to identify clear objectives and to focus their classes on teaching those objectives rather than trying to impart all of their own Internet knowledge in one seminar.

Focusing training on how to help participants achieve class objectives also helps avoid a situation where your trainers replicate their own grade school or college lecture experience in their own classes. Internet training will differ from what your beginning trainers may think of as "teaching." They need to understand that they are not merely imparting their own wisdom to others; they are facilitating the learning of their participants and providing them with practical objectives rather than theoretical knowledge. Lectures are an inappropriate method of training for public Internet training sessions.

Second, trainers need to be able to present technological information clearly and effectively. Just as they would learn in any general train-the-trainer class, potential Internet trainers should be told the importance of telling a class what they are going to teach them (the class objectives), teaching them to meet those objectives, and then telling them what they have been taught. Students learn by repetition, and since trainers will most likely see participants in only one class, they need to learn to present important points in several different ways during any single session so that those points stick in participants' minds. Trainers should also provide and review handouts that participants can take home for later study.

Part of achieving clarity lies in learning to avoid jargon and overly technical explanations. Computer experts may feel that it is important to strive for technical accuracy when explaining computer terminology and concepts to their classes. Effective trainers, however, will worry less about being completely accurate and more about getting their point across in terms that will make sense to a beginner. Do not let language become a barrier; excessive use of jargon will merely confirm a nervous beginner's fears that the Internet is too complicated and specialized for a nonexpert to learn.

If students absolutely need to know the technical terms, explain the meaning of those terms after students have absorbed the concept or provide them with a vocabulary sheet to refer to after class. In an Internet class, this will mean that trainers will be more effective when they use the term "address" rather than "URL" to refer to a web site's location, for example. After participants understand what an address is and how it is used, a trainer can then point out that another term for a web address is "URL" and that participants might run across that term when reading articles or watching shows about the Internet.

Trainers also need to be able to teach by analogy. Train-the-trainer sessions should suggest and elicit analogies for basic Internet concepts. An Internet web site address, for example, can easily be compared to a postal address—a concept that will be familiar and make sense to most participants. (This is another reason to teach the term "address" first rather than insisting that trainers use the term "URL.") Analogies can be carried through to other Internet concepts. A "404: File Not Found" message on a previously accessible site may be more comprehensible when compared to what happens when someone moves and forgets to leave a forwarding address at the post office.

People learn by metaphor, and if an unfamiliar concept can be likened to something they know, the new knowledge is much more likely to be retained. Since learners always build their own mental models to help make sense of new concepts, trainers should be prepared to provide appropriate analogies. Train-the-trainer sessions should allow time for potential trainers to create and evaluate different analogies for common Internet concepts. Demonstrate "good" analogies that are easily seen as parallel to Internet concepts, analogies that draw on concepts with which students are already familiar. The best analogies can also be extended to explain several different aspects of the medium. (Some examples of Internet analogies can be found in chapter 4.)

Most importantly, Internet trainers need to live by the old KISS ("Keep It Simple, Stupid") principle. Especially when explaining technical subjects like the Internet, trainers often have a tendency to overwhelm students by imparting too much (or simply irrelevant) information. This principle goes along with creating clear objectives for a class—trainers should be encouraged to make sure that their classes support those objectives without distracting their students with irrelevant or confusing points.

Any Internet train-the-trainer class should emphasize the fact that one common mistake of Internet trainers is to focus on the history or technical aspects of the Internet. This is one area in which your natural curiosity as a librarian or Internet enthusiast may lead you astray. While both topics may be interesting, they are inappropriate for a group of beginners whose interests lie more toward learning how to use a browser, what a web page looks like, and what sorts of things they can find or do online. History is a topic best left for reading about later, and technical aspects are best left for a more advanced group. Trainers need to remember to approach the class from the point of view of the student—to develop objectives that relate directly to people being able to accomplish necessary tasks and find information online. Avoid overwhelming students with extraneous information, or they will begin to feel that the class is either too technical for them or irrelevant to their needs.

Along with the principle of keeping it simple lies the necessity for trainers to consciously recall the steps involved in carrying out specific tasks. Remember the levels of competence outlined in the beginning of this chapter. Your "unconsciously competent" Internet experts must think back to the "consciously competent" level of expertise. In a train-the-trainer class, give trainers exercises designed to make them list each step necessary to complete common Internet-related tasks. Such tasks may include printing out a web page, performing a keyword search on Yahoo!, or using the mouse to scroll to the bottom of a long page. Have other class members follow the steps to the letter to see if they can successfully complete the task—without using any of their previous knowledge to skip ahead or fill in the blanks. In a train-the-trainer class, always allow your trainers time to practice their teaching and presentation skills on one another.

To summarize the important points to get across in train-the-trainer classes,

> define clear and achievable objectives
>
> avoid lecturing
>
> avoid jargon
>
> use appropriate analogies
>
> keep it simple
>
> don't dwell on history or on technical aspects
>
> teach skills step-by-step

Presentation Techniques

Last, trainer training classes should address appropriate styles of presentation. Although the format of classes will depend on available resources (a large-group computer-based presentation in a lab or small-group instruction around a public terminal, for example), all trainers will be giving some sort of presentation to their classes. Trainers should be provided with a list of tips for effective presentations, such as

> make eye contact with class participants
>
> ask and be available to answer questions—get participants involved
>
> don't read straight from lecture notes; be flexible
>
> convey your own excitement for the material

be prepared

practice—on your coworkers, family members, or pet, if necessary

speak slowly and with confidence, and do not condescend

keep control of time and of the session

These general training principles will help with any type of public classes in libraries. Trainers should also be encouraged to peruse books, videos, and other resources on general training and presentation skills. (Some recommendations of such resources are listed in appendix A.)

Encourage Trainer Interaction

Especially in a larger system with many trainers, your trainers may find it very valuable to have the opportunity to interact and share information with one another. Provide regular opportunities for Internet and other computer trainers to meet and to exchange teaching methods and stories. If you are in a smaller library, try coordinating a trainers' group within your consortium or among neighboring institutions.

Look for innovative ways to keep trainers' skills fresh and to keep them thinking of ways to improve their teaching style and classes. Encourage them, and provide incentives for them to keep up their skills. The Tulsa City–County Library System (TCCL), Oklahoma, for example, offers a monthly newsletter for all its Internet trainers, which is created and written by its technology instruction manager. The newsletter (see figure 2.2) combines tips for successful presentations with lists of useful and topical web sites, news about updates to the library's computers, introductions of newer trainers, and explanations of changes to TCCL's own web page. Each issue elicits feedback and suggestions for future topics from the system's trainers.

Just as attending introductory Internet class sessions will not transform beginners into experts, remember that attending one or two training classes will not magically transform people into stellar trainers. What these classes and ideas can provide, however, is a solid foundation for potential Internet trainers who will then go on to gain confidence and experience with every training session they teach.

Every trainer will need to adapt what he or she learns in train-the-trainer training to fit an individual personality and teaching style. Such sessions, however, will enable trainers to determine appropriate objectives and provide a consistent training experience to participants in any of your library's Internet training sessions

FIGURE 2.2   Internet Trainers Newsletter, Tulsa City–County (Oklahoma) Library

Internet Trainers

Tulsa City-County Library ⚘ January 2000

Training Assistance on the TCCL Web Page

Services & Collections → Computer Training & Tips

There are a number of items now on our Web page that you may find useful during your Internet workshops.

Internet Search Techniques & Tips is almost exactly like the handout we use. A few things were added for the Web page:
- Directories of Internet Search Tools
- Definitions of search engines & subject guides
- Using the **Find** function

Keyboard Shortcuts for times when it's easier to use the keyboard to maneuver around the Internet rather than using the mouse.

Printing from a Web Site maps out how to print a selected portion of a Web page by highlighting text.

Web Sites provides links to MS Office tutorial sites and **Webopedia** which is an online dictionary and search engine covering computer and Internet technology. **Webopedia** is a great resource and is searchable by keyword and categories.

Chat Tips & **Getting Started with E-mail** are essentially the handouts for the *E-mail & Chat 101* workshop. They're great for those times when you get questions about chat & e-mail that you may not have time to discuss in a regular Internet class. There are also links to chat groups and free e-mail services.

I will continue to add various handouts and information to this section that I believe you might find useful.

What additional information would be helpful for you to have in this section of the Web page for your various Internet workshops?

ISPs Scanning for Viruses

Almost all Internet Service providers have installed and are using anti-virus software on their servers. Most are updating it as frequently as daily.

Tax Information Sites

January through April are heavy tax months. If you have questions about where to find tax assistance on the Internet you may want to refer interested parties to the Business & Technology section of the Library's Web page.

Services & Collections → Business & Technology → Tax Information or *INFO Newsletter* January/February 2000 edition, section "Just look what you can find on your computer!"

In the *INFO Newsletter* issue & section listed above I've entered several good sites, including sites with information on filing electronically for both federal and state.

Sites of Interest—Discount Airlines

We've all had class participants ask about where to find cheap airline tickets on the Internet. Here's a list of some discount airlines for you to suggest.

- **AirTran Airways** www.airtran.com
An Orlando-based airline with an Atlanta hub flying to 30 cities in the East & Midwest.
- **America West Airlines** www.americawest.com
Three hubs (Phoenix, Las Vegas, Columbus) with flights into 51 cities in the U.S. and 11 destinations in Canada & Mexico.
- **Big Sky Airlines** www.bigskyair.com
Serves cities in MT, ND, WA, AR, MO, OK & TX. Call 800.237.7788 for current schedule information.
- **Frontier Airlines** www.frontierairlines.com
Denver-based with fare to 20 major cities in the U.S. Internet specials are posted Wednesday mornings and change on a weekly basis.
- **Midway Airlines** www.midwayair.com
Flies to 26 cities on the East Coast and as far west as Indianapolis.
- **National Airlines** www.nationalairlines.com
Offers daily nonstop flights between its Las Vegas hub and Chicago, LA and Dallas/Ft Worth.
- **Southwest Airlines** www.southwest.com
Serves 55 cities in 29 states and is the 5th largest airline in the U.S. Great Internet promotions.

> **FYI** 46% of the people now on the Internet are people who've just begun to use it within the last 12 months.

NOTES

1. For more on the levels of computer competence, see Elaine Weiss, *The Accidental Trainer* (San Francisco: Jossey-Bass Publishers, 1997), 4–7. The concept is also addressed in Bruce Klatt, *The Ultimate Training Workshop Handbook* (New York: McGraw-Hill Companies, Inc., 1999), 100–2, 117.

2. This grant project is described at length in Edna Kaempfer's "Training Staff and Users for Computer Literacy," *Illinois Libraries* 81, no. 3 (summer 1999): 142–51.

3

Initiating the Internet Training Program

A library's biggest challenge in developing an Internet training program for the public lies in creating classes that are both appropriate to the resources at hand and relevant to its patrons. Predeveloped, out-of-the-box classes will never exactly match a library's particular environment, and any suggestions must always be adapted to a community's unique circumstances. The format and content of training sessions will be constrained by many variables, including the level of familiarity your patrons generally have with computers, interests of your attendees, software and hardware you have available, and physical space that will be used for training sessions.

When developing a course, always be aware of available resources, of your community's needs, and of your environment. Pay attention to regular slowdowns or disruptions in Internet access in your library, no matter how minor. Such awareness can prove important to the success of your classes. Is there a surge in demand and a slowdown in response time every day at 3:00 P.M. when school lets out and children go online? If so, don't schedule a class for that time. Are your classes composed largely of senior citizens? If so, don't use the Back Street Boys official fan club site as an example during a session. Use common sense in planning classes to fit both your community and your environment.

Your training sessions will be most successful if you are able to show how Internet resources can meet the particular needs of the participants. If you are teaching a class to parents of elementary school children, for example, highlight web sites such as ALA's FamilyConnect (http://www.ala.org/ICONN/familiesconnect.html) and Yahoo's directory for younger children, Yahooligans (http://www.yahooligans.com). If you are addressing members of the local business community, show how they can use the Internet for market research or how they can post their job ads online. If you're targeting senior citizens, use investment, hobby, health, and free e-mail sites as examples. (See the next chapter for more details on designing parent/teacher classes and classes for seniors.)

Ask class participants what sorts of material they are interested in finding on the Internet. Make any Internet workshops more interactive and effective by incorporating class suggestions into your training. This means that you as a trainer should not only be comfortable with the use of the browser and with moving around the Internet but also be aware of and familiar with using one or two major sites in commonly requested topic areas such as travel, genealogy, job hunting, and so on. If a participant throws out an off-the-wall suggestion, you can either demonstrate how to do a simple search or suggest that you will be able to help that person investigate the topic further after the class.

The best way to think about making classes relevant to participants is to understand that your training has two aspects: what participants *need* to know to make effective use of the Internet and what they *want* to know about it. The latter, of course, can encompass a wide variety of possibilities. There may often be a gap between what you intend to teach in a training session and what your patrons would like to get out of a class, which makes it imperative that you maintain ability and willingness to adjust your agenda to meet the needs of your patrons.

People's time is valuable, and they will need to feel that they are going to get something out of an Internet training session that will be specifically useful to them. Even if they have not made a financial investment by paying for the class, they have still invested their time and energy in being there. Here again, library trainers have an initial advantage in that participants will have a preexisting desire to learn the Internet; they signed up voluntarily for your class. This does not excuse the obligation, however, to target your sessions toward the specific needs of your patrons.

The following sections go through each aspect of the training environment and address how to plan classes to match your library's unique set of circumstances. To help you begin your planning, start with recommendations on selecting appropriate software and hardware for use in training sessions. Then find tips on planning a class and on making training a useful experience for your patrons. Part of making sessions useful and relevant involves collecting and creating materials that will be helpful both for use during classes themselves and for your patrons as they hone their skills afterward. This will be discussed in sections on creating handouts and building an Internet reference shelf near your public terminals.

Always keep in mind that the options presented here or in other books on computer training are merely broad suggestions, and adapt them as necessary for your own library. The format and specific objectives of your training sessions will change, depending on your community and on your software, hardware, and general training environment.

Be sure to allow sufficient time to design classes and to plan and produce your handouts, notes, and other materials before initiating your program. It will be better to wait until you are ready to offer classes than to rush an unfinished program in an attempt to meet demand. You may wish to gather some input ahead of time about what your patrons would like to learn about the Internet by creating a simple survey and distributing it in the library. (See figure 3.1.) You can also use such a survey to gather basic information about what level of computer comfort you might expect from participants—ask, for example, if respondents have ever used a computer with a mouse.

FIGURE 3.1   Internet Training Questionnaire

1. Would you be interested in attending a free introductory Internet class at the library?

   ____ Yes   ____ No

2. What two specific things would you like to learn in such a class?

3. At what time would it be most convenient for you to attend an Internet training session? (check one)

   ____ Morning   ____ Afternoon   ____ Evening   ____ Weekend

4. Have you ever used a computer with a mouse?   ____ Yes   ____ No

5. What additional ideas and comments do you have for us as we begin planning our classes?

Thank you for your input!

Planning your introductory classes will require a great initial time commitment from your trainers. Once that basic structure is in place, however, modifying it to add topical or additional special classes (discussed in chapters 4 and 5) will be a much simpler process.

CHOOSING AND USING SOFTWARE

Before planning your classes, you will need to choose the software products you will make available for the public in your computer lab or at the public terminals and the software products that will help you design class handouts or computer presentations. Approach software provision for the public from the point of view of your patrons; find out what will be helpful to them as they learn and as they practice on their own after a training session. Relatively minor adjustments in the software provided may help your patrons make better use of Internet resources. If there is no word processor available on your public Internet terminals, for example, allow them access to a built-in editor such as WordPad (or the Macintosh equivalent) for taking notes and so they can copy and paste information from web sites into one document for saving or printing. Put a direct link to one of these editors on the computer desktop, and include basic instructions near the public terminals for pasting Internet material into a document and for switching between the editor and the browser.

The following sections will help you decide on appropriate software for both patrons and Internet trainers. They include suggestions on choosing and using browser software and plugins, presentation software, and security software.

Browsers and Plugins

This may seem self-evident, but many libraries forget to make sure that their public Internet workstations are all standardized using the same software. Of course, standardization is imperative during a training session itself, but is also essential as patrons strike out on their own on your public Internet terminals after attending a class. Don't offer access to Internet Explorer on some terminals and Netscape Communicator on others, and avoid mixing machines running text-based browsers such as Lynx in with your graphical workstations. By the same token, when you upgrade your browser software, upgrade it on all of your stations. This is especially important when the upgrade reflects major changes such as those between Netscape Navigator 3.0 and Netscape Communicator 4.5.

Although it may seem useful in principle to offer your patrons a choice of browser software, this will create a training and support nightmare for staff and will unnecessarily confuse patrons. For most purposes, it will be irrelevant which browser you choose to install. If your staff has become accustomed to using one type of browser, though, install and use that product on patron terminals as well. Be sure that you have a very good justification if you choose to switch browser products because you may have a revolt on your hands from staff and patrons.

If your library does change browser version or type, go through all your handouts and other materials to ensure that they reflect that change. You want any navigational handouts to resemble every public screen as closely as possible. Issues such as the fact that the buttons on the Netscape toolbar change in size and appearance between versions 3 and 4, or on the Internet Explorer toolbar between versions 4 and 5, may seem minor to a seasoned Internet user. "Minor" issues such as these will be completely confusing to the Internet novice, however. The change between Netscape Communicator and Internet Explorer will be even more drastic, and it should be avoided unless it becomes essential. Not only do toolbar buttons and file menus look different in the two browsers but the buttons are even in different places on the toolbar. (See figures 3.2 and 3.3.)

You will want to keep up with commonly used browser plugins such as RealAudio and Shockwave. Error messages asking web page visitors to upgrade to a newer version of such helper applications are both annoying and confusing to newer users. You will also want to avoid a situation in which patrons want to view a movie or other plugin-supported item and they either try to upgrade plugins themselves or ask public services staff to do so on the spot.

FIGURE 3.2   Netscape Communicator Toolbar, version 4.72

FIGURE 3.3   Internet Explorer Toolbar, version 5

Security and Antivirus Software

Check to see if your library uses security software on its public PCs. (It should!) If you have a teaching lab, install the identical security software on the computers in there as well. Configure the software so that buttons and commands always respond (or are disabled) in the same way. Your security should only be turned off for a class such as Windows 95/98 basics, in which participants need to learn the use of the Start button, My Computer, and other options commonly blocked by security software.

Choosing and implementing security software is a topic in itself and beyond the scope of this book, but common products for libraries include Fortres (http://www.fortres.com) and WinU (http://www.bardon.com/winu.htm). You may also want to use Windows NT security settings or some of the built-in Netscape options (depending on your own software setup) to make your public stations more secure. The Web4Lib e-mail discussion list for Internet librarians is a useful resource for getting recommendations on security software and instructions for creating a secure environment on public PCs. Information on joining the list and searching its archives is available online at http://sunsite.berkeley.edu/Web4Lib.

Your library should also invest in a good antivirus package for all the computers in the building. Although security software that prevents patrons from running or installing software on public machines will also help prevent infection, you will want to have additional measures in place. The presence of antivirus software will also help you reassure nervous patrons that the library has taken some precautions on their behalf. Major software packages in this area include Norton Antivirus and Network Associates' VirusScan.

Presentation Software

Beyond the software available on your public PCs, you have a choice of a variety of software products that will help you and other trainers in designing presentations or handouts. While teaching a class, it may be helpful to use some type of presentation software to illuminate the demonstration portion of the session with a computer "slide show." Microsoft PowerPoint is the most popular program of its kind for creating such computer presentations. The full program can be purchased either individually or as part of the Microsoft Office suite of products. (Although this suite is expensive, as a public, academic, or school library, your institution qualifies for an academic pricing discount.)

The PowerPoint viewer itself is freely distributable and can be copied onto any computer off of the Microsoft Office or PowerPoint CD-ROM or downloaded and installed from Microsoft's web site. Therefore, you need to purchase only one full version of the PowerPoint software to use in creating your presentation and then install the free viewer onto the computer you want to use for your demonstration. The viewer software will allow you to view and print only previously created presentations and will not permit you either to create or to edit files—so try not to count on being able to make any last-minute changes on the computer you will be using for the presentation.

A computer presentation will be most effective if you are giving your class in a computer lab or in a meeting room, using either a projection unit and pull-down screen or a large-screen TV that enables everyone to see the screen at once. You could also show your presentation to a small group using an individual PC, however, and combine the demonstration portion of your training session with lecture and hands-on instruction.

If you are teaching in a meeting room or computer lab, check out the room before the session. Make sure that the computer and projection unit (or TV) are set up. If you are using the type of LCD panel that sits on an overhead projector, make sure that you have an extra overhead bulb handy and that the screen is in focus before the class begins. It may be helpful to create a checklist and run through it before each presentation to help avoid any surprises (or panic). On your checklist, include items such as cables, extension cords, extra bulbs, enough handouts, and chairs for all the participants. Have software such as the browser and the PowerPoint viewer already loaded on the demonstration machine.

Speaking of panic, PowerPoint or other presentation software will also be useful if your Internet connection goes down in the middle of a class session, as you can still go through with the demonstrative part of your workshop. When creating slides in your presentation software, include screen captures of a variety of web sites to illustrate your presentation. In this way, too, participants will at least get an idea of what a site looks like if there are unforeseen technical problems.

To create such screen captures in Windows 95/98 or on a Macintosh, press the Print Screen key (usually near the top right of the keyboard) to copy a picture of the current window onto the Windows or Macintosh clipboard. That screen capture can then be pasted directly into your slide. Print Screen, however, creates a fairly low-resolution image. If you want sharper pictures for your slides or handouts, you can use a low-cost program such as SnagIt for the PC (http://www.techsmith.com) or ScreenShot for the Macintosh (http://www.beale.com). These screen capture applications allow you to specify a higher resolution for image captures and include other helpful options such as "capture with cursor" and the ability to capture only part of a screen.

Another advantage of software such as PowerPoint is the ability to use it in conjunction with Microsoft Word to create handouts that incorporate both your created slides and an area in which your students can take notes during your presentation. (See figure 3.4.) You can also use such software to make signs explaining the use of the browser toolbars and to create other handouts for classes or for your public stations. Be consistent in the types of visuals and fonts you use in your presentation, signs, handouts, and tutorial web pages. This will help tie all of these elements together and reinforce learning.

FIGURE 3.4   PowerPoint Handout with Space for Notes

Slide 1

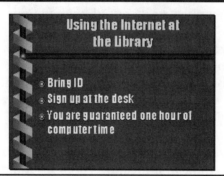

The majority of your Internet students will learn best visually, and a presentation accompanied by handouts they can read and take home will reinforce the concepts you are trying to teach. Visual aids will greatly increase the retention of class material for most of your participants. Internet trainers are fortunate in that the Internet today is such a visual medium. Demonstrating sites themselves is often the most effective way of reaching visual learners. A lecture about the Internet would be dry, indeed—the medium demands a graphic and interactive approach. Another large percentage of your participants will learn best by listening, so combine your visual presentation with lecture and explanation. A combination of verbal presentation, visuals, and hands-on practice will best help all of your attendees to learn.

Other presentation software includes Corel Presentations, which is part of its WordPerfect suite of office productivity software products. Corel Presentations functions much like PowerPoint and may be a more cost-effective solution for smaller institutions. For Macintosh aficionados, AppleWorks 6 now also includes presentation software. If your library chooses not to purchase or use presentation software, with a little effort you still can use almost any word processing program to create handouts, brochures, and signs. Include copies of images of pertinent web sites using the same Print Screen or screen capture software methods mentioned previously.

CHOOSING AND USING HARDWARE

Hardware and software go hand-in-hand, and in both cases it is advisable to purchase the most up-to-date product your institution can afford. Tempting as it may be, try not to allocate older or flaky equipment to the public or for use in a computer training lab. This will only increase the frustration level of your patrons and trainers (as well as public services staff pressed into service as tech support) when loading and browsing time is slower or when things inevitably go wrong.

Here again, remember the importance of standardization. If you have a computer lab, avoid combining Macintosh and PC-compatible computers in the same room, and certainly never use them both in the same training session. You want to make the use and support of the machines as simple as possible, and staff and patrons will appreciate needing to learn only one system. If you use laptops during training, try to purchase identical models with the same sort of mouse, with the on/off button in the same place, and so on. Libraries using laptops also might consider purchasing external mice or keyboards for them so that patrons can become accustomed to using the same type of equipment that they will see on public Internet stations. Consistency is important for beginners, and it will help them remember what they learned during a training session.

If printers are shared, especially if they are on an A/B switch, make this very clear through visible signage. Also, explain and demonstrate the use of the switch during Internet class sessions. Think like a beginner, and emphasize any aspect of the computer or of the network that may seem unusual or unclear.

Projection Options

Purchasing a projector unit or large-screen TV will allow you to use software such as PowerPoint to display computer-based demonstrations to larger groups of people than would otherwise be possible. You can also use such a system to demonstrate web sites "live" to large groups. Although purchasing this additional equipment may be too costly for smaller institutions, larger libraries or groups of libraries may wish to invest jointly in an overheard LCD projection panel or stand-alone projector unit for giving computer demonstrations to large groups. A similar option is the purchase of a special computer card that enables a PC to be connected to a large-screen TV for presentation purposes.

Whether your library chooses to invest in a projector unit, LCD panel, or large-screen TV, investigate your options for presentation hardware very carefully. Web sites such as Presentations.com (http://www.presentations.com) can provide reviews and price comparisons of different models. Strike the balance between price, performance, and portability that is appropriate for your library or system.

LCD panels that sit on an overhead projector are generally much cheaper than stand-alone projector units, but they will not produce the same brightness or image clarity. Some things to look at when choosing a projector or LCD panel include

lumens (brightness) of your unit   This will be especially important if you are presenting in a large or bright room.

ease of use   Is it more important to you that the unit has more features or that it be easier for trainers to set up?

portability and durability   If you are sharing one unit across a system or consortium, you want to choose a lightweight and more durable machine that can stand up to the demands of travel.

expected lifespan   Look here at both the expected life of the unit itself and of its bulbs, which can be surprisingly expensive components to replace.

Although the price of projector units can be prohibitive, consider splitting the cost with other neighboring libraries or urging your consortium to invest in one unit that can then be shared among its members. Since the projector unit will only need to be used for computer class sessions, some creative scheduling and cooperation will allow several libraries to share the same machine. If you intend to share a projector unit, you will want to invest in a smaller, more portable machine—although that will result in a concomitant increase in cost. Ask your vendor if there is a discount for educational or government institutions.

Investing in a large-screen television set might be a more effective option for smaller libraries. They can then also add a VCR to their setup and use the TV to show videos during programs such as staff in-service days and children's programs. Your library could also make the set and VCR available to community groups using the meeting room.

ESTABLISHING THE TRAINING ENVIRONMENT

So, your institution is already equipped with a walled-in computer lab, twenty student stations, and a teaching terminal hooked up to the latest in projection technology? You are one of the lucky few. The teaching environment is established, and your next step is to create classes to fit that available space.

If yours is like most libraries, however, you'll be starting from scratch to create your classroom or have one that is somewhat less well equipped. In that case, following are a few avenues to consider, ranging in cost from the smallest initial outlay to the most elaborate of plans. The training environment you create will in itself determine a large part of the class format, so spend some time examining your options.

Your environment will also affect the length of your class sessions. Practice and time your class ahead of time and then allow extra time for questions and digressions during an actual class. Newer trainers often have a tendency to overplan and to try and present too much material in one session. Remember that an actual class will always progress more slowly than a practice session, and allow for that when creating your agenda or outline.

A thirty-person training session in a computer lab will necessarily differ greatly in format and style from a five-person training session in front of one public terminal. The objectives of your class, however, should remain constant. You need to teach patrons to accomplish the same tasks, regardless of environment. Pay no attention to books and articles that proclaim that you must have a computer lab and state-of-the-art presentation technology to teach Internet skills effectively. You don't! There are hundreds of libraries around the country proving that with the proper planning successful Internet training sessions can be provided in almost any environment. It is always better to provide training in the environment you can afford than to throw up your hands and decide that because you lack a lab and presentation technology you will be unable to provide any Internet instruction at all.

There are several different levels at which your library can make an initial investment in creating the training environment. Following are three general options, presented in increasing order of cost. Each has its advantages and disadvantages, which are also outlined here.

Lowest Initial Investment

Financially strapped institutions may face all they can handle in paying for Internet access and equipment itself, let alone a state-of-the art training facility. The 1998 NCLIS study mentioned previously found that nearly one half of "public library outlets" (main and branch buildings) with public Internet access had just one multimedia workstation available for patron use.[1] Although some inroads have been made, many smaller libraries still provide public access or graphical access on just one or two terminals. If your institution is among these, your easiest (or only) training option is to cluster patrons in small groups around one or two public Internet terminals and teach your class sessions out on the library floor. Bring over some chairs, and let your participants arrange themselves so that they all can see the screen comfortably.

Be sure to close the other nearby Internet terminals to public use during a class session, even if your class will not be using all of the stations. The minor inconvenience to your Internet patrons is worth being able to avoid having your class participants and regular users disrupting each other and will also help dissuade kibitzers. Post your class schedule prominently so that your regular Internet users can plan their visits around your training sessions.

If you are teaching in this situation, limit your training sessions to no more than four or five participants each. You want everyone to be comfortable, to be able to see the screen, and, ideally, to get a bit of hands-on experience. Switch off and have each student control the mouse and keyboard for at least part of the session, and at the very least, make sure that each person gets a chance to practice scrolling up and down the screen and clicking on links. Your students will not truly feel that what you have taught them is valid until they have had a chance to try it for themselves.

You may find that you are more comfortable demonstrating the use of the browser yourself than allowing participants to control the computer during a class, or you may find your classes populated by absolute beginners whose lack of keyboarding or mouse skills slows down the session too much. In this case, you can do your demonstration and then allow time afterward for hands-on practice. Remain nearby and available for questions or further demonstration.

The main advantage to this small-group approach for your library is obviously its cost-effectiveness. You can use existing resources, and one trainer can handle each class. Another plus is that you will be conducting training on the identical machines your clients will later be using. As mentioned earlier, beginners will benefit from consistency, and getting used to using the usual public terminals during a class is a helpful way to start.

Your patrons may also appreciate what you can bill as "the personal touch." Beginners will be less intimidated by small-group sessions and more comfortable asking questions and otherwise participating during a class. Trainers will be able to give more individual attention to each participant, and students will be more able to get to know you in a smaller, more informal setting. Small-group sessions strike a comfortable balance between formal lab classes and individual instruction and will more easily enable you to develop a rapport with your students.

On the negative side, no matter how quiet you try to be, classes will inevitably be somewhat disruptive to other Internet users and other library patrons. Other patrons may interrupt your session or object to the public terminals being blocked off. Furthermore, although demand for class sessions may be high, only a few patrons can be trained at one time, and it is more difficult to give each participant hands-on experience if they do not each have their own station. Also, training will seem less official to students when presented outside a computer lab or classroom environment. Students may not take classes as seriously or may be in less of a "learning mode"—which will present a special challenge to you as a trainer.

Medium Investment

Many libraries would like to offer larger and longer training sessions than are practical when teaching a class at public workstations located on the library floor, but they don't have the resources for a fully equipped computer lab. If yours is among these institutions, consider doing the lecture/demonstration part of your class in the library's meeting room and then moving out to public Internet stations for hands-on practice in the main part of the library. Be sure to block out time on the public stations and to end the presentation portion of the session on time so that machines will be available for your group to use.

An effective Internet demonstration will require the use of a large-screen TV or projector unit/panel to present your program. Students can then learn by both listening and seeing. Since the Internet is such a visual medium, it will make much more sense to participants when you can actually demonstrate web sites during a presentation. Consider investing in a projection unit, or look into borrowing one from your consortium.

In this case, you will merely need to move a computer into the meeting room for the presentation portion of your training session. Keep one of your computers on a rolling cart or desk for easy mobility, or use a laptop during presentations. You should also preferably run an Ethernet line or equivalent connection to the room so that you can quickly connect a computer for a real-time demonstration. This is where presentation software such as PowerPoint will be most useful, especially if you are unable to run an Ethernet cable to the appropriate point.

Give some thought to how you will set up the chairs in the room that will be used for presentations. An overhead projector and LCD panel can often block the view from many locations in the room, as can other students' heads and computer monitors. Make sure that each seat has a clear view of the pull-down screen or television set and of the trainer. (Room layouts will be discussed further in the next section.)

Combining presentation and hands-on practice during one class session will be helpful to participants, who will then have a better idea of what the Internet looks like and how to move between sites before they are expected to touch a machine themselves. Make sure to present your demonstration portion first and to allow plenty of time for each portion of the class. This is a good format for a ninety-minute class that allows around forty-five minutes for presentation and forty-five minutes for hands-on practice. Leave some time for a short break in the middle to give participants a chance to stretch their legs and refresh their minds before beginning the hands-on portion of the session.

Highest Investment

The highest initial outlay for your institution will be if you choose to build a computer lab in which to teach your Internet and other computer classes. This, however, will only be feasible if your library has both the space for a lab and the money to purchase the necessary computers, peripherals, and software. Also remember that the presence of a lab will require additional staff time and training on everything from signing patrons in to maintaining the equipment. Always plan for ongoing costs with any technology project, especially when building a large-scale project such as a computer lab.

This is one instance in which finding grant money can be essential for smaller or more financially strapped institutions. A number of libraries have benefited from programs such as the Gates Library Initiative, for example, which can provide the initial funding to build a fully equipped computer lab—filled with computers running Microsoft software. The Tulsa City–County (Oklahoma) Library System's Martin East Regional Library is a typical example of a Gates-funded project. In December 1999, the library received a ten-computer lab from the Gates Initiative. The lab includes one trainer PC and a 36″ monitor for use during presentations. It can be used for staff and patron training and is otherwise open for public use. Your library may be eligible for a Gates or similar grant that will help it construct a computer lab, so investigate all of your options before dismissing the possibility outright.

Using a lab for training sessions causes the least disruption to other library users and will allow the most opportunity for hands-on practice. Most computer training manuals, too, assume a lab situation, so you will be able to make better use of their suggestions if your environment more closely matches those assumptions.

Your patrons will also take classes much more seriously when they are taught in a lab environment. The use of a lab makes your training sessions appear more like a "real class," and sitting in a lab will help some of your participants automatically snap into a learning mode. The downside of this is that these more "official" class sessions may be intimidating to some of your patrons, especially Internet beginners who may be more comfortable with a more personal and unstructured approach. You might consider offering both large lab classes and small, more individualized sessions if staff and time permit.

If you do build a lab, spend some time designing it with the needs of Internet and other computer classes in mind. As mentioned previously, be sure that computer and overhead equipment does not block the view from any of the stations. Whatever configuration you choose for your lab must be useful during class sessions and during daily use by patrons. Remember that the constraints of running power and network cables may mean that the configuration that you initially choose will be a configuration you will be committed to for quite a while. Don't feel compelled, however, to use the traditional rows of desks—experiment on paper or by moving desks around before installing the actual computer equipment and connectivity. See which configuration best suits your space and your training needs. Figure 3.5 shows three possible configurations for computer labs.

FIGURE 3.5 Possible Room Layouts for Training

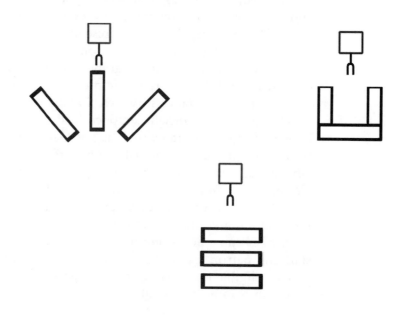

In your computer lab, instead of using a projection solution, you might examine the feasibility of using a networked display in which the contents of the instructor's screen are displayed on each student's monitor. This, though, can also be a somewhat expensive solution. In addition, this encourages participants to pay attention to their own screens rather than focusing on or interacting with the instructor. Individual PCs can be distracting in any lab situation; it can be hard for a trainer to compete with the tempting and colorful screen sitting right in front of each participant. Remember also that a room full of computers will be somewhat noisy, and practice projecting your voice over the hum of all those fans.

PLANNING AN INTERNET BASICS CLASS

Once you have your training setup in place, it is time to start planning the format of your classes. Determine how long your sessions will be. Generally patrons will be willing to stay no longer than two hours at a stretch for a basic session and may prefer one that is closer to one hour. Limit yourself to what can effectively be covered in that time period. Limit yourself to the truly important objectives, and avoid overwhelming students with too much or extraneous information. It is better to cover the basics thoroughly than to give participants so much information that no one can remember anything about what was said during the class.

At this point, it will be helpful to go back to the section in chapter 2 on training-the-trainer classes, which covered ways to present technical information effectively. Remember the importance of creating clear and simple objectives for training sessions. Never assume that your students will have any previous knowledge. (For a specific discussion on teaching absolute beginners, see chapter 4.)

Content

Just as you should create a list of core competencies for general staff and Internet trainers, you should also create a similar list for your Internet class participants. List the objectives for the class, deciding what participants will be able to assimilate in a given session. Remember from chapter 2 that objectives (or outcomes) are measurable or observable. They encompass concrete and specific skills that you want participants to learn. You are teaching students how to complete particular tasks rather than imparting abstract knowledge. Knowledge may be picked up as a result of training, but training needs to focus on concrete objectives. Sample objectives for an introductory Internet class include the ability to

> type in an Internet address to go to a particular web site
> click on an underlined or image link to move to a linked web site
> use the mouse to scroll up and down the page
> use the back and forward buttons
> see if a site is secure before putting in a credit card number
> print out a web page

Following is a very simple outline of a one-hour introductory Internet class using Netscape Communicator.

Introduce self, pass out handouts, ask students briefly about computer experience (have they used a mouse?), briefly mention process for signing up, and explain participants can do so after class. Tell participants to feel free to ask questions throughout the class. 4 MINUTES

Go through handouts, explain what they contain and how they can be used after a class session. 3 MINUTES

Explain that Netscape is the software ("browser") used to look at web pages. Mention that there are others, but that Netscape is used in this library. 2 MINUTES

Show students how to type an address (URL) into the web address bar. Explain how it is analogous to a postal address and always goes to only one particular place on the Internet. 3 MINUTES

Show how the background of the Netscape icon keeps moving and the bar on bottom moves while the web site is still loading. 1 MINUTE

If students are unfamiliar with the mouse, show how to scroll up and down the web page (make sure you choose one that is more than one screen) by using the bar on the right-hand side. 3 MINUTES

Use the site to demonstrate clicking on links. Encourage students to watch for the cursor turning into a "little hand." 4 MINUTES

Show the use of the back button. Show how the forward button lights up once students have gone back. Go back and forward a few times. Then show how to use the home button to go back to the library's home page. Explain how the home page may be different on different sites, but in the library it will always be this particular page. 5 MINUTES

Explain other pertinent toolbar buttons. Show how to print, and explain that it will print all the way to the bottom of the web document, not just what is currently visible. Explain that the stop button can be used when a site is painfully slow. Explain that they will probably never use the reload button but may want to sometimes on places such as news sites, that it will go get a fresh copy if things have changed a lot since the site was first loaded. Pick an e-commerce site, pretend to buy an item, and show how the security button can be used to see if there is security on a site (the lock closes up and turns bright yellow). 8 MINUTES

Demonstrate the use of the search button, and explain that this is the easiest way to search. Do a simple search. Mention that there are other ways to search. Mention that it is best to be as specific as possible when searching because there is so much information online. 7 MINUTES

Ask for questions and summarize class content. 5 MINUTES

Provide time for hands-on practice. Remain available to answer questions and help students navigate. 15 MINUTES

Avoid getting locked into your outline, lesson plan, or notes—be flexible and leave room for some give-and-take with participants. Any outline is just a guide to what you need to cover, and it is fine if topics get out of order, if some take more or less time to cover than planned, or if minor issues are left out. Just ensure that participants have a chance to learn and practice each class objective. Flexibility is especially important if participants turn out to be either more- or less-advanced than anticipated. You want to avoid either boring students or talking over their heads.

When creating objectives, remember that you are just teaching the basics. No introductory class can cover everything a participant may ever need to know about the Internet. Your job is to provide participants with the basic skills they need to continue on their own. Help participants generalize the specific skills you show them so they can apply them to other computer and Internet situations. Show them during class how skills are transferable; for example, clicking the *x* at the upper right corner of a Windows program *always* closes the software, whether in Netscape or any other program.

What **not** to Do

"Thou shalt nots" for a basic training class include the following:

> Thou shalt not focus on the history of the Internet. While interesting, this is time-consuming and irrelevant to a beginning user.
>
> Thou shalt not get too technical. In a basic class, attendees are not going to assimilate or care how information is transmitted—they just want to know that it is.
>
> Thou shalt not neglect to leave time for hands-on practice.
>
> Thou shalt not assume knowledge that your class does not have.

Common sense will take you far!

TRAINING AIDS

Any training class will benefit from the use of handouts and other materials that will help clarify the class objectives. This is especially true in the case of Internet and other computer classes, in which the use of the software is not especially intuitive. These materials are a simple way to add value to your training classes and to extend the impact of your sessions by providing a ready-reference resource for participants. Libraries will also want to make some material available near their public Internet terminals for general patron use.

Cheat Sheets and Handouts

Many resources on computer training stress the importance of "cheat sheets"—brief handouts that participants can use after they have completed the training to help them carry out tasks important to their job. (You may also see these referred to as "job aids" when perusing manuals on how to train others.)

In a library training environment, however, you don't have the luxury of identifying learners by job title or knowing exactly how people are going to use Internet resources. Again, it is important to adapt information from commercial training programs (most of which assume a business environment) to the library situation. Although you do not know that a patron is going to come away from Internet training needing to complete specific job-related tasks, you do know that there are common needs that can be met. Cheat sheets can be helpful in extending the amount of information you are able to provide. In most situations, you will have very limited time available for classes, and students may not have long to practice on their own. Cheat sheets give them the tools to practice after a session and help explain peripheral topics that cannot be covered in one class.

On a public Internet station, for example, there will be a demand for printing out material to take home. Do you charge per printed page? Consider making a cheat sheet that explains step-by-step how to print only part of a document, an aid that will be welcomed by your more cost-conscious patrons. (An example of such a handout for Netscape Communicator can be found in appendix B. This will be less of an issue if your library uses Internet Explorer, which allows visitors to print only a selected portion of a page.) Also use cheat sheets to explain exactly how to carry out such basic tasks as saving and bringing in one's own bookmarks, saving a file to disk, copying pictures to disk, or cutting and pasting text into a word processor file. Make these cheat sheets available by all your public Internet terminals.

Make sure that a person following the steps listed on each cheat sheet is able to complete the task successfully. Give the instructions to someone unfamiliar with the Internet or with computers (enlist a new staff member, a willing patron, or a family member) and have them try to complete the task using only the information on that sheet. Label each cheat sheet with a clear, large header, so that patrons glancing through your handouts will be able to locate the one that meets their needs as quickly as possible.

Make cheat sheets clear, short, and concise. Avoid jargon. Recall any difficulty you yourself may have had in the past with following the directions in software manuals, and avoid repeating those mistakes. Use bulleted lists or labeled screen shots rather than full sentences whenever possible. You are trying to give instructions on how to accomplish a task rather than provide the philosophy behind each step. Leave out any extraneous information. Also, think about how most people use those software manuals. They never read them straight through but use them to look up how to accomplish a specific task when they need to know how to do something. Your cheat sheets should cover these most common "need to knows" without distracting patrons with the rest of the verbiage software manuals need to include.

Providing cheat sheets in the library presents a perfect opportunity to create giveaway bookmarks (yes, the old-fashioned kind). Use the front and back of card stock cut to bookmark size to list the appropriate steps in carrying out common tasks. People will be more likely to use and keep the cheat sheet if it is a handier size than the traditional 8½″ × 11″. Be sure to print on both sides of the bookmark so that patrons at your Internet stations do not just use them for scratch paper.

As previously mentioned, software such as PowerPoint can be used to create handouts that incorporate copies of your slides or screen shots with space for taking notes. During class sessions, you also may wish to hand out copies of your library's Internet policy, definitions of Internet terminology, and so on. Give attendees some material to take home to remind them of what they learned during a training session. If you have a large number of handouts, color-code them for easy reference during a class. Tie class handouts closely to your outline, following the same topics in the same order as they will be presented during a session.

Make a note of the Internet resources most commonly used by visitors to your public-access Internet terminals. Is there a demand for free e-mail services such as Hotmail or Yahoomail? Are individuals regularly looking up phone numbers, searching for a job, researching the stock market? Create handouts that list and describe Internet sites in these areas.

Creating not only cheat sheets and other handouts but lists of resources, an addition of links to your library web page, and so on will enhance the training and the Internet experience for many of your patrons. Look into options such as purchasing clear mouse pads into which you can insert a sheet detailing how to search for information online or how to use the library's home page. Search for unique ways to get information in front of your Internet users and class participants.

Make sure that any handouts are readable. Resist the temptation to continue making photocopies of copies until you are left with an eighth-generation sheet of gray fuzz. Also, spend some time making handouts visually attractive. You are teaching a class on using computer resources; show your participants that you know how to use a computer to lay out handouts with plenty of white space, clear and large fonts, and appropriate visuals. Use only one style of clip art, and be sparing with its use. If an image is worth a thousand words, imagine how cluttered too many pictures will make your handouts appear. Often the only art you may need on a handout will be labeled screen shots explaining how to use the software and demonstrating applicable web pages.

These same principles apply to any PowerPoint slides or web pages you create for use during training sessions. Strive for clarity above all else, and avoid cluttering any of your visual or learning aids with extraneous information.

Books

Consider setting up an Internet reference shelf near your patron-access terminals. Include books on the use of your browser software, guides to Internet resources on specific topics (think: genealogy, job-hunting, government resources), Internet yellow pages, and so on. Keep this material up to date; if you switch browser versions, don't keep guides to older installations by the terminals. Internet users will appreciate having references close at hand.

HINTS FOR A SUCCESSFUL PROGRAM

Trainers can take several concrete steps to help ensure the success of their training sessions. First, be sure to revisit and practice your examples on the day of the class—sites tend to move and servers tend to go down. Make sure all of your Internet addresses are correct, and beware of relying entirely upon your own memory. One hapless librarian had this lesson brought home during a public training session when inadvertently mistyping the URL http://www.dogbreedinfo.com (a helpful site listing different dog breeds and their characteristics) into the browser and accessed an "adult" site.

To help avoid such situations, trainers can use their own notes to remind them of useful web addresses and points to cover during a class. Especially if you have several trainers, though, your library should consider creating a class outline for use during all training sessions. (An example of such an outline is provided in a previous section. This will provide a consistent training experience to all patrons and help ensure that trainers are teaching the same objectives during each class. The outline should never be a word-for-word script but, rather, should provide an ordered overview of the objectives that will be covered during each class. For another sample outline or script for trainers, see Berkeley's "Introduction to the World Wide Web and Netscape," at http://www.lib.berkeley.edu/TeachingLib/Guides/Internet/pt1scrpt.pdf.

Again, do not neglect the small steps that will help classes go smoothly. Number the pages of your outline or notes. If they should happen to get knocked onto the floor in the middle of a session, you do not want to spend precious class time shuffling them back into order. An outline, whether on paper or in your head, can also help you keep a session on track and on time. Try not to keep participants longer than advertised. Wear a watch or make a habit of checking the clock on your PC.

Use browser bookmarks or a simple page of links to access specific sites quickly and easily during a session. You can make the links page available to students as well, especially in a lab situation. Just set your page as the home page for your teaching computers during a session, and you can easily take a few minutes after the class to set the home page back to its original default.

Using Computer Presentations

Some tips for creating computer presentations were given in the earlier section on selecting presentation software. After you have created a presentation, however, you need to practice presenting your program to a class using the actual computer technology. Many trainers make the mistake of hiding behind technology, either literally or figuratively. If you use a computer presentation, make a special effort to interact with class participants. The use of computer technology makes it easy to fall into the trap of hiding behind the PC monitor and lecturing to students rather than engaging with them. You may believe it will be less difficult for you as a trainer to teach if students are unable to see you, but you will be detracting from your own effectiveness.

Also be sure to keep the information on the screen short and to the point, elaborating on it by talking with participants and asking them questions. Focus on your students rather than on the screen. Even during the presentation portion of your session, interacting with students is essential. Try not to lecture to them. They are not your "audience," they are participants in the session and responsible for their own learning.

Focus less on creating a jazzy presentation and more on presenting information in a straightforward and simple manner. Avoid using technology for technology's sake; use it to enhance what you are able to teach. The drawback to using software such as PowerPoint is that it will be easy to get carried away with the computer's abilities to create animations and blinking lights. Ad designers have ensured that the web itself will be distracting enough in this way! In introductory Internet classes, always look at your computer presentation as a supplement to your session rather than as a replacement for interaction and hands-on practice. (Demonstration-only sessions may be appropriate later when showing topical sites to a group already familiar with the basic use of the Internet.)

Interacting with Students

Pay attention to your students. Do they look lost? Are they reluctant to ask or answer questions? Try to gear your class to the proficiency levels of your students, and make sure that you have created an environment in which they are comfortable participating. Emphasize that if you use terms or concepts with which they are unfamiliar, they should feel free to ask for clarification. Never assume either that they will be familiar with any particular computer term or that their silence means that they are following your every word.

Try to build a rapport with your group. Even in a short, one-time session, you can make eye contact with your students, interact with them, and make an effort to remember their names. Tell them yours. Start the class off by introducing yourself so that your students know whom they are dealing with. Sometimes small things like taking the time to interact with participants at the beginning of a class session will make the difference between a successful learning experience and a disappointing class.

Encourage participants to interact with you and with each other. This is one reason it can be very helpful to ask questions and to elicit questions from participants. Try to ask not only yes-or-no questions but more open-ended questions that can help you elicit longer and more thoughtful responses from participants. This will help them think about what they have just been taught and will involve them in their own learning. In a beginning class, even asking participants for a topic they would like to search for helps get them involved.

Be prepared to deal with the different types of "problem students" that may emerge in any class. You may have participants who feel too advanced for a basic class and compelled to demonstrate their boredom or their intolerance of others' questions or who are ready to take over and prevent you (or anyone else) from getting a word in. You might have attendees who come to a class prepared to challenge the library's Internet policy. Or you may have patrons who proclaim that they only came to learn "one thing," such as how to buy plane tickets online, and who project their impatience with all other parts of the class.

You begin to see why any Internet trainer needs to possess patience. Be prepared to tell a student that you will be happy to deal with a particular issue after the class, but do not allow any individual participant to hold up an entire session with his or her agenda. You can also use the "after class" method if a participant asks you something you don't know. Neither make something up nor ignore the question—you will lose credibility and the trust of your participants. Tell them you will try to find an answer after the class or you will get back to them. No one expects you to know everything, and students will be more suspicious of a trainer who prevaricates than of one who forthrightly admits ignorance in a particular area.

Ask specifically for comments and questions from other, quieter participants. You can use and demonstrate sites in the participants' areas of interest during the class, but no one student should be allowed to dominate the entire session. It is your responsibility as a trainer to keep control of the session so that all participants are able to learn. Try not to get dragged into arguing with or focusing on just one person. As you teach more classes, you will become accomplished with dealing with all sorts of different personalities.

Expect to see patrons of varying skill levels in your classes. This will be especially true if your library offers only one introductory Internet class rather than a series of sessions of varying levels of difficulty. Some participants will merely need some guidance as to what they can find online, while others will need to learn specific basic skills such as the use of the mouse.

Ensure that each participant experiences some level of success during your class, whether this lies in finding some piece of useful information online or successfully using the mouse to click on a hyperlink. Successes will vary depending on the initial skill levels of the patrons attending your training session. Some may be happy just learning in one session how to use the mouse to move the pointer around on the computer screen.

Scheduling

Schedule classes to meet the needs of your library patrons. When will participants be most able to attend training sessions? Seniors, for example, may not like to go out at night. Business professionals might appreciate a "brown bag lunch" session. Children need to be out of school. Offer a variety of time and day options so that patrons with other obligations will have more opportunities to attend, and avoid scheduling classes near major holidays or other events. If possible, get names and phone numbers of students in case a class needs to be rescheduled.

Striking the right balance as to the frequency of classes will be more complicated than setting up appropriate schedules. You need to consider the staff that will be available to teach and the potential demand for training sessions. You want to avoid a situation where classes fill up immediately and potential students are turned away, but you also want to avoid wasting staff time by requiring trainers to teach sparsely attended sessions. Some experience will let you find the proper balance after a few months. Common sense will tell you to schedule extra classes, though, if you do a big advertising push. Also schedule additional sessions in January and February if possible—the holiday season is a traditional time for people to buy new computers and many of your patrons will be discovering the need to learn more about the use of their gifts.

CONTINGENCY PLANNING

What are you going to do when your connection at some point inevitably goes down during a class session? Consider various backup possibilities such as using PowerPoint slides, having handouts ready, and saving some web sites on disk before your session. As mentioned earlier, a computer presentation that incorporates images of web sites, while less interactive than you may prefer, will still give participants some feel of being online and allow you to continue with the class in case of unforeseen outages.

Also examine computer programs such as WebWhacker for Windows and for Macintosh http://www.bluesquirrel.com) or SurfSaver (http://www. asksam.com, for PCs only) that allow you to download the text and images of entire web sites to your own hard drive. Plan ahead and use WebWhacker or SurfSaver to copy a few sites to your computer prior to your presentation. You can then demonstrate the feel of being online and the look of certain web sites even if your connection goes down. Using such software also lets you turn to saved web pages complete with graphics and clickable links if your connection is slow or a site is temporarily unavailable.

Allow for the possibility of equipment failure as well. Audiovisual equipment is notoriously temperamental; just imagine what happens when you add computers to the equation. If you incorporate computer presentations into your training sessions, have the PowerPoint (or equivalent viewer) loaded onto more than one PC so that a presession hard drive crash or other failure will not paralyze you. If equipment fails during a class, try to get it going again, but do not devote an inordinate amount of time to troubleshooting.

If your Internet connection or electric power goes down prior to the class, consider rescheduling the session. This means that when participants sign up for class sessions, you should get their names and phone numbers in case of such an event.

ADVERTISING THE PROGRAM

Begin by advertising your Internet training program as you would advertise any other library event: through your library's newsletter, brochures, and signs. Send a press release to the local paper. (An example of a press release can be found in appendix B.) Call the paper to find out to whom you should send the release; most papers will accept press releases by fax. Always double space your press release, and print it in an average size font on white paper or on institutional letterhead. At the top of your release, include a suggested headline that will tell editors the main subject at a glance. Offering Internet classes gives your library the opportunity to attract a new group of patrons who may not have been regular library users in the past; many members of your community may even be unaware that the library offers Internet access.

Another advertising idea is to post a prominent notice on the start-up screen on the browsers at your public terminals. Library visitors who may soon realize they are in over their heads in trying to use the Internet on their own may notice the availability of classes when they first sit down at the computer.

Make any advertising appropriate for your expected audience. Signs and brochures advertising classes for beginners should use a round, friendly font such as Comic Sans MS and maybe some cartoon clip art. Material promoting classes for business professionals should use a more professional font such as Times New Roman. Computer classes are also an area in which patrons will be looking for professionalism and knowledge—misspellings or other minor errors will detract from your ability to project that image.

COMPUTER-BASED TRAINING

Computer-based training (CBT) will be discussed here only briefly as a possible supplement to formal class sessions. CBT refers to online self-directed training sessions or tutorials. This method of training is becoming more popular in business settings as a way of reducing training costs. CBT, although a growing field, is not necessarily an appropriate option for libraries—whose strength, as always, lies with the ability to interact with people. CBT lacks that personal touch and can be frustrating for newer users whose questions go unanswered if they have not been anticipated in advance.

One difficulty with CBT is that it requires a basic familiarity with technology before it can even be used. Learning how to use the Internet *on* the Internet or on a PC is somewhat difficult without some prior knowledge of how to move around in the medium. Staff members or patrons who want to supplement their Internet training with additional self-study might turn to computer tutorials, but these training aids are not yet a replacement for hands-on teaching. CBT does, however, allow for additional self-directed learning after a class at a student's own pace and schedule.

CBT encompasses a variety of possibilities, but one of the simplest options for libraries is merely adding an Internet tutorial to an existing library web page. A large number of Internet tutorials from companies, individuals, and other institutions can be found online. You may want to list some on your library's web page or to include them as resources for further study in your class handouts. Avoid linking to an independent tutorial site in such a way that you give the impression that the site was library-created, and be careful to check the date the site was last updated. Some recommended online tutorials for beginners are listed in the next chapter. Also, consider creating your own online guides. You can tailor these to explain the details of Internet use in your particular library, and they will provide a handily available reference for patrons to go back to after a training class. Be sure to update these as you change the browser version or type you use in your library, however.

Visit some online Internet tutorials from other libraries. Libraries that have created their own online tutorials include the Gary (Indiana) Public Library, whose tutorial is online at http://www.gary.lib.in.us/internet_tutor.htm, and the Baltimore County (Maryland) Public Library, which has posted a four-part Internet tutorial on its web site at http://www.bcplonline.org/tutorial/tutorial.html. Figure 3.6 shows the first screen for the Baltimore County Public Library's Internet tutorial.

Some libraries have posted the PowerPoint presentations used during their public Internet classes onto the web. PowerPoint offers an easy way to convert presentations into large image files for use on web sites, but these can take some time to load from home or on a slower Internet connection. Such

FIGURE 3.6
Baltimore County (Maryland) Public Library's Online Internet Tutorial

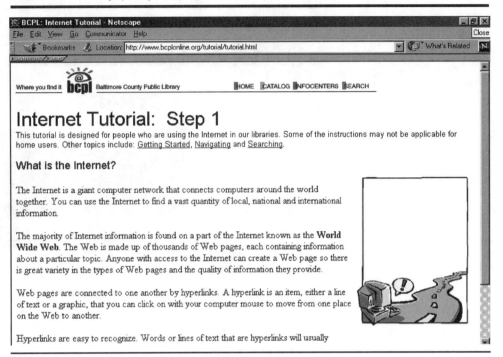

presentations online, furthermore, fail to take advantage of the interactive capabilities of the web, and the use of the built-in navigational controls can be cryptic for a newer user. Also be careful that your presentation is viewable both in Internet Explorer and in Netscape Communicator; PowerPoint has a tendency to be Internet-Explorer specific.

Libraries might consider posting their presentations on their web sites as a supplement to classes because of the ease of getting such presentations online and because the slides will already be familiar to students who have completed a class. Examples of online PowerPoint Internet tutorials can be found on the web page for the Toledo (Ohio) Public Library at http://www.library.toledo.oh.us/internet/i_tutorial.html and on the web page for the Enfield (Connecticut) Public Library at http://www.enfield.lib.ct.us/enfield/cyberspace.html. (See figure 3.7.)

Whether you choose to post a PowerPoint presentation, link to others' tutorials, or create your own web-based tutorial, providing such information on your library's web page will help your students progress on their own after class sessions. Make any tutorials simple and friendly to use; they can be a helpful supplement to the books, handouts, and other resources your library can provide to facilitate learning. Provide many different types of resources to help your patrons become independent learners and continue using the Internet on their own once their formal Internet instruction has ended. Always mention to students that support will be available in all these forms, and even though they have completed the class, they should not hesitate to ask for additional clarification from you in the future.

FIGURE 3.7
Enfield (Connecticut) Public Library's Online PowerPoint Presentation

Slide 1 of 18

Some libraries may want to expand their program of Internet instruction, and ideas for doing so can be found in the next couple of chapters. When creating any such additional classes, however, remember to plan out specific class objectives just as you would for an introductory Internet session.

NOTE

1. U.S. National Commission on Libraries and Information Science (NCLIS), *Moving toward More Effective Public Internet Access: The 1998 National Survey of Public Library Outlet Internet Connectivity* (Washington, D.C.: US NCLIS, 1999). Available: http://www.nclis.gov/what/1998plo.pdf.

4 Teaching to Diverse Groups

Libraries can add some variety to their Internet class offerings and make them more specifically applicable to their community by providing public training sessions geared toward particular groups. Any Internet training program should take into consideration both the diversity of your library's community and the particular needs of your patrons. All members of the community deserve the opportunity to learn about the Internet, especially as familiarity with its use is becoming a prerequisite for using many library services. Following, therefore, are some suggestions and resources for developing classes that target several unique user populations and some examples of how other libraries have proceeded in creating their own classes. Included are ideas for creating Internet training sessions for absolute beginners, native Spanish speakers, parents and teachers, and the elderly.

Each section describes the process of selecting trainers, designing classes, and creating advertising materials for the respective group class. You will also find some recommended resources to help in planning such sessions. No library should feel compelled to replicate these specific ideas. You can use them, however, to guide you in developing similar programs in your own library, or you may modify them as necessary to create programs for teaching other major groups in your local community.

You may not need to schedule your targeted group classes as regular events. Depending on the staff you have available and on patron demand, classes for particular groups can be planned as special events or as a supplement to more general Internet classes. Look at these sessions as a way to reach out to diverse groups of patrons, and consider offering them as part of larger programs planned around specific occasions. Spanish-language classes, for example, would be a natural addition to a Hispanic Heritage Month calendar of events, while classes for beginners or for parents and teachers would be a good supplement to your National Library Week "Read! Learn! Connect! @ the Library!" program.

TRAINING BEGINNERS

Librarians who are accustomed to using the Internet every day may underestimate how intimidating the very idea of getting online can be to a computer beginner. Learning the Internet is like learning any new skill. Few people start out being completely comfortable with or skilled at driving a car, cooking a meal, or solving an algebra problem, so why should we expect them to have an innate knowledge of and comfort with computers? Even experienced users are often confused by some aspects of the Internet, so consider how much more perplexing (or even downright scary) common online events such as a "404: File Not Found" message, seemingly random search results, and "illegal operations" will be to newer users.

Yet, if your institution takes the extra time to teach computer and Internet skills to beginners, these patrons can become some of the most enthusiastic supporters of your Internet program. The mere fact that you reach out to computer beginners who may be either too intimidated or financially constrained from receiving computer and Internet instruction elsewhere will enormously raise your institution's credibility and value in their eyes. Public services librarians are often especially good teachers of computer and Internet beginners because they are already used to cultivating patience in responding to all sorts of inquiries from library patrons.

Furthermore, providing Internet and other computer classes for beginners will help reduce the time your public services staff needs to spend providing tech support for library users. Patrons who have a basic foundation in computer skills will be able to make more effective use of the library, and librarians will be more able to focus on connecting users with information. Formal classes should reduce the time librarians need to spend in piecemeal explanations of each basic computer skill every time a patron needs to accomplish a task such as using a mouse to click on a link or printing out a page of citations from the online catalog. This will reduce aggravation for everyone. It also helps avoid situations in which computer-illiterate library visitors seek individual tutoring from a staff member who personally may not be very sure about the technology.

Selecting Trainers

Trainers who will be teaching classes composed of absolute computer or Internet beginners will need to be strong in several of the personal qualities mentioned in chapter 2, particularly patience, enthusiasm, and people skills. They must be willing to let beginners take the time to learn at their own pace and must be able to resist the urge to take over a machine and "do for" a newer user. If you are the only Internet trainer in your institution or if there are only one or two trainers available, remember and practice these important attributes. Nothing will intimidate a beginner more than a trainer who goes too fast, expects participants instantly to remember class content, and gets impatient and takes over when a user seems to be moving too slowly or fails to remember the exact sequence of steps necessary to complete a particular action.

Trainers of computer novices must be able to avoid jargon without becoming condescending and be able to convey enthusiasm for the subject without getting ahead of the group. In short, trainers of beginners need to possess the same personal qualities as do all trainers, but in somewhat larger doses.

Above all else, trainers of beginners need truly to believe that beginners are not stupid and to understand that computer use is not intuitive. Both you and your students need to trust that students can learn and have faith in your ability to teach them.

Designing Classes

Everyone starts somewhere, and many of your patrons who are curious about the Internet may have had little or no practice in such computer basics as the use of the mouse. You may wish to consider identifying absolute beginners by describing Internet class prerequisites or by offering a self-evaluation form (as described in chapter 2). Try to provide computer novices with a separate introductory class or give them some preclass, hands-on practice with resources such as the Washoe County (Nevada) Library System's web page that introduces the use of the mouse. (See figure 4.1.)

Stories (although some perhaps apocryphal) abound about computer neophytes who pick up a computer mouse and point it at the screen as if it were a remote control or who, when told to "right click" on an icon, pick up the mouse and use it to try to write the word "click" on the screen. (Also remember to explain the term "icon," which may be completely unfamiliar

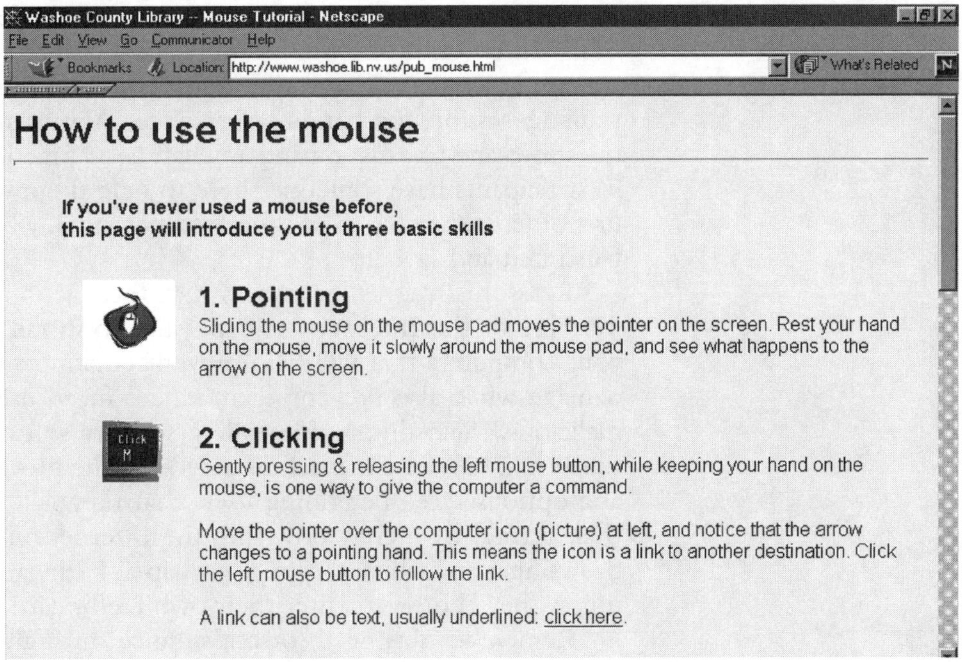

Figure 4.1   Washoe County (Nevada) Library System's Mouse Tutorial

in the computer context.) Unfamiliarity with the mouse need not be dramatic to be recognized as a major obstacle to effective use of the Internet. Not being able to use the mouse well will not only prevent your patrons from using the Internet well, it will also cause them intense frustration and create negative feelings toward the library as a whole when they are prevented from accomplishing a task as supposedly simple as looking up a book in a web-based OPAC.

Making the correlation between the movement of the mouse on the mousepad and the cursor on the screen is one thing; assimilating the hand-eye coordination necessary to control the movement of the mouse cursor and to hold the mouse steady while clicking is a skill in itself. Patrons might find some mouse-related tasks somewhat easier if your library invests in "scroll" mice, which have a small top wheel that lets users scroll up and down the screen without either having to click and drag on a bar or to click on the tiny arrows on the sides of the screen. It also may be helpful to slow down the cursor and double-click speeds on computers for beginners.

Present mouse basics first. You might even want to introduce your class to a simple game such as Windows Solitaire, which will be easier to do if you are in a computer lab and have machines available for each participant. Let them spend a few minutes getting the hang of pointing, clicking, and dragging in an entertaining way before moving on to more advanced skills. Computers also will appear much less intimidating when displaying a familiar sight such as a row of playing cards. (If students are not familiar with the game, provide an alternative activity such as the online mouse tutorial mentioned earlier.)

If staff and time permit, your library can offer beginning computer classes in topics such as basic Windows 95/98 in addition to its introductory Internet training sessions. When patrons are already familiar with such computer basics as using the mouse, opening and closing programs, and cut-and-paste, they will already have a leg up on, and be less fearful of, the intricacies of the Internet. If offering multiple classes is not practical in your institution, be sure at least to allow some time at the beginning or end of each Internet training session for hands-on practice. Always remain available to answer questions and to assist during any hands-on practice sessions. It will be better if participants have someone there to help them when they get stuck for the first time. If they try to use the Internet initially by themselves, they may get frustrated and give up.

Reassure Internet beginners that their actions will not break either the machine or the Internet itself. Be sure to install security software on all of your computers that will help prevent beginners from inadvertently causing damage while also preventing more advanced users from being deliberately malicious. (Selecting and installing security software is beyond the scope of this book, but see the brief discussion in the previous chapter for some hints and options.) Tell beginning users that they will be unlikely to compromise their privacy by merely browsing the Internet on a public machine and that browsing also will not sign them up for unwanted products and services unless they choose to enter their own credit card number when prompted.

Remember this need for reassurance throughout the class. If a program running on Windows 95/98 machine should crash, for example, take the time and opportunity to explain that the unfortunately named "illegal operation" error does not mean that the user did something wrong. If a Macintosh displays a bomb on the screen, you will similarly need to reassure your participants that computer designers are overly dramatic, that this is not their fault, and that "things like this happen all the time." Emphasize this. Newer users are often terrified that their experimentation will hopelessly destroy the computer, when a willingness to experiment is often the best way to learn. Try to create an environment in which beginners can become more comfortable with the machine and will understand that unexpected results are not necessarily due to anything that they did. Computers misbehave! Try to help beginners have a good first experience with computers so that they have the desire to use them in the future.

While you are helping beginners become comfortable with the computer during a class, remember that it is also important when teaching computer novices to provide them with handouts and "cheat sheets" to refer to when a class session has ended. No beginner will become expert in using the Internet after merely one or two classes, and your participants will need material to look back on to jog their memory later. People learn by doing, and many of your class participants will be returning to practice using the Internet on their own, pursuing their individual online interests. Create handouts that picture, label, and describe the function of each button of the browser's toolbar, for example. (See the previous chapter for a more detailed discussion on creating outstanding handouts.)

In addition to the importance of handouts, remember the power of analogy. Although your participants will be unfamiliar with Internet concepts, they will be familiar with other analogous media and situations. During a session, you might compare the computer, for instance, to a television set. Whatever brand you choose to buy, your TV will be capable of picking up all of the different programs—the main difference being that, on the Internet, most "programs" (web sites) are "on" all the time, rather than being shown on a set schedule. Your browser software then works somewhat like a cable converter box, transforming signals into viewable content. If you don't have a browser, you can't decipher the content. Also, as with television programming, you have to put up with a lot of advertising to access the actual content of Internet sites.

Depending on your audience, web sites can also be compared to magazine articles. The targeted advertisements that appear above and within search results or on topical web pages are much like those in fashion magazines, for example, where an article on makeup tips will be accompanied by a full-page ad for lipstick. Beginners will be more comfortable with the technology when they understand that, while the medium may be new, the concepts are very similar to those in the traditional media with which they are familiar.

Comparing the web to television or to other common technology will have the added advantage of helping to put class participants at ease. Point out that, for example, while most of your audience will be licensed drivers, few may understand exactly what goes on under the hood of a car. People are used to interacting every day with technology without necessarily becoming expert (or wanting to be) in its inner workings. This is another reason that trainers should avoid focusing on overly technical information; make class content appropriate to your audience. You are not training a group of mechanics; instead, you are teaching basic driver's ed. If your students are intrigued by the Internet and interested in learning more advanced concepts, they can go on to do so, but this is not your purpose during an introductory session.

For your class of beginners, also be sure to create a list of objectives for the session. Start by identifying what a beginner needs to know before Internet instruction will make sense. For instance, they will need to be able to use the mouse and will need to be able to open and close the browser software. From there, identify the basic Internet concepts that can be taught in the time available for your session. It may be possible to present only a few concepts in your beginners-only class, and participants can then go on to take other classes after becoming more secure in the basics.

In one class session beginners can be taught how to click on an underlined link to get to another Internet site; how to use the back, forward, and home buttons in the browser; and how to type in a URL to go to a specific web site. These basics will provide a foundation for either further self-study or additional formal instruction. Remember that your primary role as an Internet trainer is to facilitate learning. Your goal in training beginners is to help them gain a solid foundation of basic computer and Internet skills that will enable them to learn and progress in the future.

As a supplement to group sessions, libraries with sufficient staff may consider providing the option of scheduled one-on-one Internet instruction for beginners on an appointment-only basis. Such sessions can be helpful for beginners reluctant to attend classes and display their lack of computer and Internet skills in front of a group. Scheduling one-on-one, hands-on instruction also ensures that a staff member will be available to provide uninterrupted assistance, unlike what usually occurs when staff are asked to provide help on a walk-in basis while also continuing to keep an eye on the reference desk and an ear out for the phone.

Advertising

Advertising for the classes offered for computer and Internet beginners should stress that these introductory Internet classes will be geared toward absolute novices and that no previous computer or Internet knowledge will be assumed. Many of your patrons may be interested in learning about the Internet yet hesitant to sign up for a training session because they are unsure of their own computer skills and feel as if everyone else in the class will be more advanced. Advertise that classes will be taught using plain, simple language with a minimum of computer jargon.

Emphasize also that classes for beginners will be taught in a nonthreatening manner with plenty of opportunity for hands-on experience. In addition to publicizing the availability of beginners' sessions in your library's newsletter and through press releases to the local paper or radio station, also put up signs in the library. Have a sign by the Internet terminals, but also put signs in prominent locations by the reference and circulation desks. In this way, those who have been hesitant to approach the library's computers will be exposed to your advertising in their everyday interaction with the library. (See appendix B for a sample press release and an example of library signage.)

Resources

Many helpful resources exist for trainers planning classes and for newer computer users independently learning Internet skills. Those mentioned in the following discussion are a starting point in creating your own classes.

When planning training sessions for beginners, it might be helpful to ask for suggestions on an e-mail discussion list for Internet trainers for example, NETTRAIN. Subscribe to NETTRAIN by sending an e-mail message to listserv@ubvm.cc.buffalo.edu. In the body of your e-mail message, leaving the subject line blank, type: subscribe NETTRAIN (insert your first and last name). The list's archives can be searched at http://listserv.acsu.buffalo. edu/archives/nettrain.html. Search for keywords such as "beginner," "novice," and so on. Periodic discussions on the list cover strategies for teaching beginners, and many experienced trainers have offered tips and suggestions.

Books for computer and Internet beginners abound. Your library should stock at least a few of these titles, and you can consider adding some to your Internet shelf by your public terminals and having several on hand at any class session for beginners so that they can check them out. In addition to books on Internet fundamentals, include books on computer and Windows or Macintosh basics as well. Internet beginners are also often computer beginners, and they will need practice in basic computer skills before working on mastering specific Internet techniques. Recent helpful titles for computer and Internet beginners include Joe Kraynak, *The Complete Idiot's Guide to Computer Basics* (Indianapolis: Que, 2000); Nat Gertler, *Easy PC's: See It Done, Do It Yourself* (Indianapolis: Que, 1999); and Reader's Digest, *Get Online!* (Pleasantville, N.Y.: Reader's Digest Assn., 1999).

Also look at web sites for computer and Internet beginners, and provide a printed list of or online links to some of these so that your patrons can use them for reference and self-study purposes. Make sure, though, that the examples and instructions on the sites you recommend match the brand and version number of the browser software you use in your library. As mentioned previously, a variety of groups and individuals have posted Internet and computer tutorials online, and some of these sites are freely printable and distributable by nonprofit organizations such as libraries.

Examine and include sites such as Internet 101 at http://www2.famvid. com/i101/internet101.html (see figure 4.2), and WebNovice at http:// www.webnovice.com. You may also want to recommend a site such as Webopaedia at http://www.pcwebopaedia.com, which provides searchable definitions of computer and Internet terms.

FIGURE 4.2   Internet 101

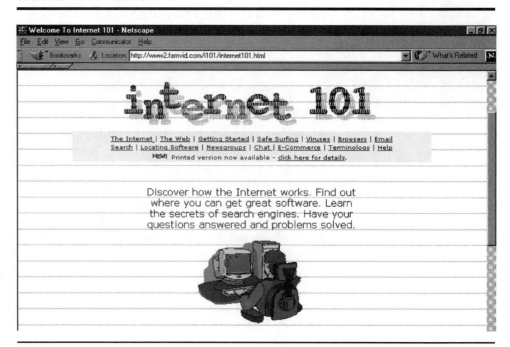

Copyright 1997–2000, Scott Cottingham

TRAINING SPANISH-SPEAKING PATRONS

Many public library communities contain large numbers of patrons whose native language is not English. Although the following ideas and examples focus on helping you design Spanish-language Internet training sessions, they are easily adaptable to other non-English-language classes as well. Spanish-language classes are specifically described here because in many communities libraries are experiencing an increase in their number of Spanish-speaking patrons. Use the descriptions as a model upon which to base non-English classes that are appropriate for your community.

Some members of your local Hispanic/Latino community will be more able and likely to use the Internet if information is presented to them in their native language. Providing Spanish-language Internet classes is an important step toward making library services and information available to all in communities with large Spanish-speaking populations.

Start by establishing the need for Spanish-language instruction in your community. Use census results or population surveys to determine the number of Spanish-speaking residents. Anecdotal evidence will also be helpful; note, for instance, if you have had a large number of patrons requesting Spanish-language classes (or materials) and using your terminals to visit Spanish-language Internet sites. Your library might also create a Spanish-language version of the Internet training questionnaire provided in the previous chapter. Add a question to determine respondents' country of origin, which will help you plan classes that incorporate pertinent resources for your local Spanish-speaking community.

Also examine publications such as the National Telecommunications and Information Administration (NTIA) 1999 "Digital Divide" report, which notes that Hispanic/Latino households in the United States are around one half as likely to own a computer than are white households, and are 2.5 times less likely to use the Internet.[1] The report also notes that Hispanic/Latino Internet users tend to use public access points such as schools and libraries for their connectivity. This creates a need for libraries with large Latino/Hispanic populations to offer their patrons Spanish-language Internet classes. Such libraries might also consider creating English and/or bilingual classes with a cultural component.

Libraries serving a large number of Spanish-speaking patrons, furthermore, may be eligible for grant money to develop their technology training programs and infrastructure. See, for example, the information on the federal matching funds TOP (Technology Opportunities Program, formerly TIIAP) grant. A description of the TOP grant process is available online at http://www.ntia.doc.gov/otiahome/tiiap. Another possibility is the Library Services and Technology Act (LSTA) grant, which is generally administered by the state library in each state. Grant money may also be used to hire bilingual staff to either teach classes or translate for other trainers.

Selecting Trainers

Ideally, if your library is located in a community with a large population whose native language is Spanish, one or more staff members will reflect that community and be fluent in the language. Bilingual librarians can then either teach Internet classes themselves or, less optimally, serve as translators for your usual Internet trainers.

Especially in communities whose demographics have been changing rapidly, your institution may not have bilingual staff members. Your bilingual staff may also be uncomfortable serving as Internet trainers. In this case, consider working with community volunteers, using them either as teachers or as translators. (Ideas for and examples of general volunteer trainer programs can be found in chapter 6.) Also, it may be feasible for your library to create a cooperative arrangement with neighboring libraries that have Spanish-speaking staff members, or you may be able to pay a Spanish-speaking librarian from a neighboring library to provide instruction at your institution on a per-class or per-hour basis. Least optimally, you may find it necessary to contract out Spanish-language Internet instruction entirely. Have an outside agency translate your own class materials into Spanish, and let them use your materials or class outlines to teach classes at your institution or make an agreement to allow an outside agency to present its own Spanish-language classes at your library using your equipment.

Designing Classes

As with any Internet training program, design classes with the needs and interests of the participants in mind. Know your community. Some libraries with Spanish-language Internet programs have had good results when they

FORT BEND COUNTY LIBRARIES

Explorando Internet

Hay 2 grandes sistemas de navegación (o navegadores) en Internet. Uno de ellos se llama *Netscape,* el otro *Internet Explorer.* Por el momento, cuando visites cualquier sucursal de las Bibliotecas del Condado Fort Bend, vas a encontrar *Netscape Navigator* como navegador.

En Internet, puedes buscar:

> Direcciones exactas, por ejemplo
> **http://www.colmex.mx**

> Nombres de compañías e individuos, por ejemplo
> **Houston Comets**
> **Gloria Estefan**

> Conceptos, por ejemplo
> **poesía**
> **beisbol**

Para direcciones exactas y nombres de compañías e individuos, hay que usar un buscador como los siguientes:
- **AltaVista**
- Excite
- Hotbot
- Yahoo!

focus on resources available from their participants' country of origin. For example, in a class composed largely of Mexican immigrants, you might demonstrate how to locate and read articles in online newspapers from Mexico. Also explain how to use Spanish-language e-mail sites to communicate with family members in other states and countries.

Look at your existing English-language handouts and cheat sheets and see how they might be modified. Often, handouts can simply be translated, although you will wish to replace examples and URLs of specific web sites with their Spanish-language equivalents. Figure 4.3 shows part of a brochure advertising a Spanish-language Internet class.

If your library has a web page, provide a separate page of links to some pertinent Spanish-language sites such as those mentioned in the resources section later in this chapter. Include news sites, search engines, Internet tutorials, and so on, as well as links to information of local interest. Libraries with larger Spanish-speaking populations may provide additional online information in Spanish, such as program descriptions and other library information.

Design your Spanish-language Internet classes much as you would your English-language Internet basics training sessions. Create a similar list of objectives but use topical Spanish-language web sites as examples during the class. You should be able easily to modify your introductory outline to teach the Internet to Spanish-speaking patrons.

Advertising

Libraries offering Spanish-language Internet training have come up with many methods of announcing the availability of their classes. The Tippecanoe County Public Library in Lafayette, Indiana, for example, publishes class information in the Spanish supplement to the community newspaper, distributes it through in-house flyers and flyers distributed to local Hispanic/Latino businesses, and disperses brochures through Spanish-speaking social workers and community leaders. The Riverview Branch Library (St. Paul, Minnesota) offers Internet and computer classes in Spanish and Hmong and uses similar methods of publicizing its sessions as well as advertising on Spanish-language radio stations.

Any advertising ideas must be adapted to your library's budget and resources. Though this may seem obvious, be sure to promote Spanish-language classes in Spanish. Make bilingual flyers. Be creative in your approach, and post some bright, eye-catching flyers in nontraditional locations such as local grocery stores, churches, and community centers. Emphasize that these training classes are free.

Librarians who teach such classes also stress the necessity of moving outside the library, using other community institutions to help advertise the availability of computer training sessions in Spanish. As Kirsten Serrano, who teaches Spanish-language basic Internet and e-mail classes at the Tippecanoe County (Indiana) Public Library, notes: "Go to the Latino community leaders to advertise. The best advertisement is word of mouth." Make sure that community agencies that serve the local Latino/Hispanic population are aware of the availability of your Internet training program, infect them with your enthusiasm for it, and let them advertise for you. This will be a much easier process if your library has a history of cooperation with community groups. Rather than looking at your Internet classes in isolation, consider your training program as being one integral component of your library's mission of service to its community.

Resources

A variety of resources can be helpful when beginning to plan out your Spanish-language instructional sessions. Use the following books and web sites as you proceed, and never forget the importance of networking with other librarians.

Learnthenet.com offers self-directed online Internet tutorials in a variety of languages (English, French, German, Italian, and Spanish). Its Spanish-language guide may be found at http://www.learnthenet.com/spanish/index.html. (See figure 4.4.) Consider providing a link to this site or to similar online Spanish-language training materials and tutorials from your library's web page or use the site as a supplement to formal classes. (Note that Learnthenet.com still shows examples using older versions of the two major browsers.)

Several libraries have collected a variety of links to Spanish-language resources on their institution's web page. These selected sites can be helpful to demonstrate as examples during classes or to use as selected resources for

FIGURE 4.4   Aprenda La Red

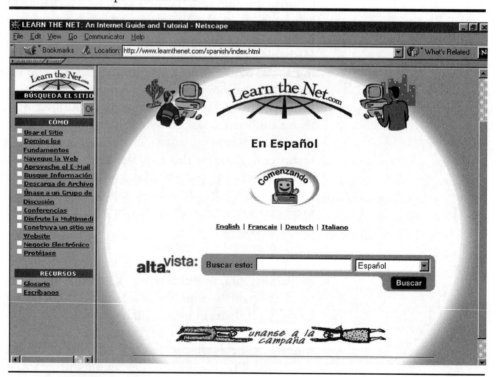

Copyright 1996–2000, Michael Lerner Productions

inclusion in your own handouts or library web page. Such library-created sites include the St. Paul (Minnesota) Public Library's Sitios en Español at http://www.stpaul.lib.mn.us/pages/pubpg/sitiosen.htm and the San Antonio (Texas) Public Library's Enlaces en Español at http://www.sat.lib.tx.us/html/espanol.htm.

Recently, Spanish-language books, audiotapes, and other materials have become much more readily available through major jobbers such as Ingram (which now publishes a yearly catalog of Spanish-language materials) and through specialty vendors such as Lectorum (info@lectorum.com). Some helpful titles include Jaime Restrepo, *Internet Para Todos* (New York: Random House, 1999), and Peter Kent, *¡Internet Fácil!* (Englewood Cliffs, N.J.: Prentice-Hall Hispanoamericana, 1998), as well as other original titles and translations of popular English-language guides (such as the Complete Idiot's Guide series) to Netscape Communicator and Internet Explorer. The information in these books may help you in planning your program or in creating handouts. If you have a large group of Spanish-speaking Internet users, you will want to include some of these Spanish-language guides on the Internet shelf by your public access terminals.

Librarians interested in getting advice from other Internet trainers serving Spanish-speaking populations should investigate organizations such as REFORMA (National Association to Promote Library and Information Services to Latinos and the Spanish-Speaking), which provides an e-mail discussion list on which librarians can network with one another. REFORMA's web site (http://www.reforma.org) also might be helpful in planning your program, as it includes relevant sections on Spanish-language search engines, Internet terminology in Spanish, and a Spanish-language guide to learning HTML. At the organization's web site you can also find information and instructions on joining its electronic discussion list.

Another helpful resource for all libraries serving Latino/Hispanic populations is Camila Alire and Orlando Archibeque's *Serving Latino Communities: A How-to-Do-It Manual for Librarians* (New York: Neal-Schuman, 1998). Although the authors do not specifically address Internet instruction, their ideas on resources for planning programs for Latinos/Hispanics, doing needs-assessment and outreach, and finding funding will be helpful as you begin to plan your Spanish-language classes.

Spanish-language web sites that will be helpful for demonstration purposes during classes and for use in handouts include resources such as search engines, e-mail services, and news sites. The following examples will help get you started:

Search Engines/Indexes

Yupi.com (http://www.yupi.com) is a Spanish-language equivalent of Yahoo!

Yahoo! en Español (http://espanol.yahoo.com) provides its own Spanish-language directory.

HispaVista (http://www.hispavista.com) is another large directory/search engine.

Free Web-Based Spanish E-mail Services

MixMail (http://www.mixmail.com) provides free e-mail and more.

LatinMail (http://www.latinmail.com) includes e-mail, chat, and classifieds.

Léttera (http://www.lettera.net) is another option for web-based e-mail.

News

MundoLatino (http://www.mundolatino.com) gives news from across the world with a Latin American emphasis.

CNN en Español (http://cnnenespanol.com) is CNN's Spanish-language edition. It is smaller than the online English version and updated less frequently.

El Nuevo Herald (http://www.elherald.com), from Miami, is a good source for news about Latin America.

You may also mention the still-rudimentary free web page translation services now available online, such as AltaVista's translator at http://babelfish.altavista.digital.com. Be sure to supplement the listed sites with Spanish-language resources from your participants' countries of origin or from your local community.

English and Bilingual Classes for Latinos/Hispanics

Remember while developing your Spanish-language Internet training program that many U.S. Latinos/Hispanics may not be Spanish speakers yet will be interested in cultural information available online in English. Again, the principle here is to make classes relevant to the participants. Consider offering English-language or bilingual Internet classes for the segment of your Latino/Hispanic population that is not fluent in reading Spanish.

In such classes, focus on English-language and bilingual sites of cultural interest. U.S. Latinos/Hispanics may maintain a strong interest in their own countries and culture, and owners of Latin American web sites have long noted that a large portion of their traffic stems from the United States. Such a cultural class would be a natural project for a featured Hispanic Heritage Month or Cinco de Mayo program, for example.

TRAINING PARENTS AND TEACHERS

As mentioned in chapter 1, parent and teacher classes can be a useful forum for explaining the benefits of Internet access in the library and clarifying your own library's Internet policies to members of your community. Look at classes for parents and teachers as an opportunity for the library to present the usefulness of the Internet to children, letting you demonstrate resources for homework, learning, and making connections with other students online. Parents, especially, will often welcome information on useful Internet sites and practical tips for online safety that help counteract the sometimes hysterical portrayal of the Internet in the popular press.

Selecting Trainers

Given the prevalence of such sensationalistic portrayals, however, it is especially important when planning a class for parents or teachers to select a trainer who is enthusiastic about the potential of the Internet and who is able to explain your institution's Internet policies clearly. Parents may be sensitive to the presence of the Internet in the library and apprehensive about its availability to their children, so trainers should be prepared to describe the usefulness of the Internet to children, explain the library's Internet policies and its decision whether to use filtering software on public machines, and suggest ideas for activities parents and children can do online together. Trainers should be aware of how children have benefited from using the Internet in the library and be able to share pertinent anecdotes.

Trainers should also be ready to explain ways in which parents and teachers can help children protect themselves online, and resources for helping do so are described in the next section. Whatever your institution's decision and position on filtering software, its trainers will need to explain the necessity for parents to involve themselves in their children's online activities, since no filters are 100 percent effective.

Designing Classes

Classes for parents and teachers present an opportunity to describe how children can take advantage of the wealth of information available online. Demonstrate educational sites such as museums, zoos, and local community web pages and "fun" places such as Arthur's home page (http://www.pbs.org/wgbh/arthur) and Pokemon (http://www.pokemon.com) sites. Describe how children can take a virtual field trip and explore places they don't have the opportunity to visit in person. Try to match the resources presented in your training session to the grade level of parents' children or of teachers' classes. Sites appropriate for and interesting to high school seniors, for instance, will be on a quite different level than those aimed at an elementary school child.

Education is the most common reason for parents to buy and encourage their children to use computers. Show them how to take advantage of the Internet to make learning fun and exciting. The resources section lists a few examples to get you thinking about how to catch the attention of teachers and parents attending your Internet classes.

When presenting a class to K–12 teachers, describe both the online resources available at the library for children working on homework projects and ways in which teachers can use the Internet to help them in planning classroom activities and while teaching their own classes. The skill and comfort level of teachers will vary widely depending on your community, the availability of and commitment to Internet and other computer applications in the schools, and the commitment of the respective institutions to technology training for teachers.

Before planning a class for teachers, find out the details of the school's own training agenda, if any, and get copies of its handouts and class outlines to avoid duplicating those efforts. Teachers will also be interested in the many web sites offering lesson plans, curriculum development ideas, and other teacher-specific information. Depending upon their school's commitment to training, teachers may be well-versed in the basic functions of the browser software. In this case it will be more appropriate to provide them with a demonstration of useful web sites than with hands-on Internet instruction per se.

If your library has a web site, consider using it to support the local school curriculum. Create lists of recommended web resources to help children complete large projects that are assigned each year. Add topical resources according to what the schools are working on each month, which will often go along with exhibits you may have displayed in the library around events and celebrations such as Black History Month or Cinco de Mayo.

When presenting a class to parents, concentrate on activities parents and children can do together online as well as on major online parenting resources such as Parent Soup at http://www.parentsoup.com. Parents will generally be especially interested in the potential of the Internet to help their children succeed educationally.

For both parents and teachers, describe the importance of online safety for children and provide tips they can use in discussions with their classes or with their own kids. Don't avoid the issue in the hopes of making it go away; chances are it will be in the forefront of your class participants' thoughts.

Go over Lawrence J. Magid's Kids' Rules for Online Safety (see figure 4.5) or a similar list, and explain that parents and teachers can help children protect themselves online just as they give them information to help protect themselves in "the real world." Emphasize that parents and teachers need to teach children to never give out personal information online, report sites and e-mail that make them uncomfortable, never arrange to meet anyone without a parent's permission, and never believe everything that they read online. Again, analogies can be helpful here—parents can provide guidance for their children's Internet use just as they do for their television viewing.

Advertising

If you want to reach teachers, it will be important to advertise your classes through the schools and to time class sessions to take place right after the school day ends. After putting in a full day teaching, many teachers will be unwilling to come back out to the library for an evening or weekend session. If at all possible, take your class on the road and see if your presentation can be scheduled on site at the school during a free period or as part of the local

FIGURE 4.5   Kids' Rules for Online Safety

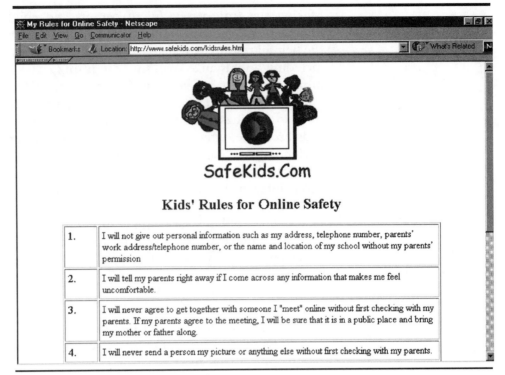

From SafeKids.com by Lawrence J. Magid.

schools' staff development day. Most schools are now wired for Internet access, so with some cooperation and advance planning you should be able to use their equipment for a class or demonstration or to temporarily hook your own laptop or PC into their network.

Again, the success of your program for teachers will depend largely on your existing relationship with the local schools. Classes will be better attended and received if your library has already developed a strong relationship with local school districts. If you have a school services liaison librarian at your institution, have him or her tout the advantages of your Internet training program to local teachers and administrators and even teach or co-teach the class sessions if possible.

You may want to advertise classes for parents through the schools if you have a positive relationship with the local district. See if teachers will allow you to distribute brochures to be sent home with the children. If your relationship with the local schools permits, consider offering Internet demonstrations to parents as part of a general parent orientation at the school. Offer to demonstrate topical sites to the local PTA. Also advertise in the children's section of your library's newsletter, send a press release to the local paper, and describe the program at storytimes and other library programs where you have a captive group of parents already present. If your library has a web page, advertise the class on your own site, and be sure to demonstrate the youth services component of your site during parent and teacher training sessions.

Resources

Making the Internet useful to parents and children is one area in which librarians and library organizations have been quite active. Be sure to peruse the helpful resources available online from the American Library Association, including Librarian's Workshop at http://www.ala.org/pio/cyber/cando. html, KidsConnect at http://www.ala.org/ICONN/kidsconn.html, and 700+ Great Sites! at http://www.ala.org/parentspage/greatsites. The latter site also provides a link to the Librarian's Guide to CyberSpace for Parents & Kids brochure, which can be read online or ordered from ALA for the cost of shipping and handling. Call (800) 545-2433 x4044 or e-mail pio@ala.org.

Virtual field trip, homework, and tutorial sites exist in every area of academic interest, from space travel to biology to museums worldwide. Keep in mind that many of these sites will require multimedia plugins, such as QuickTime or Shockwave, and ensure that the appropriate software is loaded on your terminal prior to your demonstration. Supplement these recommendations with sites of local interest such as those devoted to the history of your state or community.

Science

One site that should rivet budding biologists is the Interactive Frog Dissection tutorial at http://curry.edschool.virginia.edu/go/frog/menu.html.

For those who are more interested in space exploration, NASA provides a plethora of online resources for educators and students at http://education.nasa.gov.

History and Social Studies

For use in completing school projects, demonstrate sites such as the Internet Public Library's POTUS (Presidents of the United States) at http://www.ipl.org/ref/POTUS.

Amazon Interactive teaches students about the geography, people, and natural resources of the Ecuadorian Amazon at http://www.eduweb.com/amazon.html.

Museums

The Smithsonian has a comprehensive guide for teachers, including suggested lesson plans in a variety of subjects that take advantage of its resources at http://educate.si.edu.

How many students have a chance to visit the Louvre in person? They can take a virtual tour online at http://www.louvre.fr/louvrea.htm.

Many state library associations also have created their own online lists of topical sites; see if yours has created one that might include resources specifically applicable to your community. Often state-created sites for children will include links to state history sites and other local information, which can be useful homework aids. Also take a look at search engines geared toward children, such as Ask Jeeves for Kids at http://www.ajkids.com. This site is particularly helpful since it allows children to type questions in natural language and select the closest matching question precreated by the Jeeves staff.

A variety of books for parents, teachers, and children list fun and educational Internet sites of all types and explain how to use the Internet and different ways to get online. Your library should own several. When planning your class, examine titles such as Preston Gralla, *Online Kids: A Young Surfer's Guide to Cyberspace* (New York: John Wiley, 1999), and Ann Barron, *The Internet and Instruction: Activities and Ideas* (Englewood, Colo.: Libraries Unlimited, 1998).

During classes, you may want to pass out copies of brochures discussing child safety on the Internet, such as Lawrence J. Magid's "Child Safety on the Information Highway" from the National Center for Missing and Exploited Children and accessible online at http://www.safekids.com/child_safety.htm. Printed copies can be ordered by calling (800) 843-5678. Parry Aftab's recent title, *The Parent's Guide to Protecting Your Children in Cyberspace* (New York: McGraw-Hill, 2000), also addresses online safety for children in a straightforward and nonhysterical manner.

Trainers should find some useful, up-to-date statistics and information on the impact of Internet use on children's other activities. A good starting point for such statistics is the Safe & Smart web site at http://www.nsbf.org/safe-smart. This site, sponsored by the Children's Television Workshop, the National School Boards Foundation, and Microsoft, reports on a study showing that children who use the Internet spend more time reading, less time watching television, and are more interested in school.

TRAINING SENIOR CITIZENS

Depending on your service community's demographics, you may find that a significant percentage of your Internet class participants are senior citizens. Even if your library chooses not to provide separate senior-only sessions, you may find yourself teaching many senior participants in your introductory training sessions.

Many libraries have created Internet training classes geared specifically toward seniors. Some older patrons may be more comfortable learning the use of computers and the Internet in the company of their peers. Define "senior" as seems appropriate for your library. A few libraries with an Internet training program for seniors provide senior classes for people ages 50 and over, but most set the age at 60+, or at 65 and over. Remember, it is never too late to learn. A variety of recent articles and polls even describe the "graying of the Internet" because computer and Internet ownership and use among seniors is surging and beginning to approach the national average for all ages. The 55 to 74 age group, in fact, has been the fastest-growing group of both Internet users and computer users in general. Seniors have begun to take advantage of the medium and create their own communities online.

While the groups focusing on the graying of the Net are generally interested in seniors' purchasing power, the main attraction for most seniors will be the power of the Internet to bring people together and to allow them to investigate their own hobbies and interests online. Some may be interested in keeping up with their children or grandchildren. Many seniors who learn how to use the Internet mention their relief in no longer being left out when their grandchildren talk about going online. Seniors in your community might welcome the opportunity to learn about a medium that has become so pervasive in many aspects of our culture.

Like any computer beginners, seniors in your community may be intimidated at the thought of being grouped in a class with others who will come in with more previous knowledge. Some seniors also just may be more comfortable learning among their peers, and offering senior-only classes will allow you to use examples focusing on the primary interest areas of your group.

Selecting Trainers

Some groups swear by the benefits of seniors teaching their peers, while others advocate an intergenerational approach. Your library will probably be constrained in this area by available training staff, but it might consider using suitable senior volunteers as trainers or partnering with an organization such as SeniorNet (http://www.seniornet.org) to offer instruction at the library.

A common mistake of Internet (or any computer) trainers is to talk down to seniors or to assume that their age automatically precludes any knowledge of or affinity for the medium. Avoid prejudging class attendees as either technophobic or technologically inept or lumping all seniors together. Never assume that they will be less able than other trainees to assimilate technological knowledge. If you are training a class of retirees, remember that those with computers at home will have had a lot of time to experiment with and learn the machine, although they may tend to underestimate their own skills.

The special qualities needed by all trainers will particularly come into play when you are teaching a class for seniors. Especially remember to use patience, to avoid taking over a beginning user's keyboard, and not to condescend. If you are much younger than the group you are teaching, members may be especially likely to object to any hint that you are patronizing them. While avoiding talking down to senior students, also remember to avoid talking too quietly or too quickly, which is a common mistake of nervous or beginning trainers.

Your role as a trainer, as always, will be to facilitate the learning of your class participants. Your goal will be to give seniors the skills they will need to use the Internet for everything from web-based e-mail to researching topics from health to genealogy.

Designing Classes

Seniors who will be attending a basic Internet class, especially those who do not have computers at home, generally will have had less exposure to the medium than your younger adult students. Like any beginners, they may also need introductory instruction on use of the PC. However, unlike many of your other patrons, seniors may not have used a computer at work and will

Creating classes for seniors also offers a wonderful opportunity for your library to partner with other community agencies. Consider taking your classes on the road, for example, and teaching sessions at the local senior center or retirement home. The Multnomah County (Oregon) Library, for example, has an ongoing Cyber Seniors outreach project through which library volunteers bring notebook computers to local senior centers and other agencies serving seniors. There they demonstrate Internet resources, show how to use the library's catalog, and teach seniors how to use e-mail. (See chapter 6 for more detail on Multnomah's and other libraries' cyber senior programs.) Your library might also want to send trainers to speak to local senior groups and demonstrate relevant online resources.

Advertising

Again, remember the importance of word-of-mouth advertising. The best advertisement for your training program will be the testimony of a satisfied customer. Also publicize your program through community groups and institutions composed largely of seniors, such as your local senior center. Emphasize that these are seniors-only sessions. If senior groups use your library to meet or if you provide other library programs for seniors, remember the value of cross-promotion in getting exposure for your training program.

In your advertising, mention some of the many web sites of interest to seniors. Talk about what you will show them how to accomplish online. Your advertising should convince seniors that there truly are online opportunities for older adults.

Make any signs or brochures describing senior classes clear, legible, and uncluttered. Again, strive for legibility and clarity above all else.

Resources

Recently, several books have begun to address the senior computer user, including Mary Furlong, *Grown-Up's Guide to Computing* (Redmond, Wash.: Microsoft Press, 1999), which unfortunately, although aimed at older readers, uses a very light typeface; Abby Stokes, *It's Never too Late to Love a Computer* (New York: Workman, 2000); and Richard A. Sherman, *Mr. Modem's Internet Guide for Seniors* (Alameda, Calif.: Sybex, 1999). Add such titles to your library's collection, and use them to gain ideas for your training classes by perusing their recommended web sites for seniors, accessibility tips, and so on.

Most of these guides discuss general computing and online subjects from a senior's perspective. A section on finding travel information online, for example, may discuss how to find Elderhostel information in addition to providing information on more general sites such as Travelocity and Microsoft Expedia.

Also examine and demonstrate web sites designed for seniors interested in learning more about technology. One example is AARP's Computers and

not have grown up with one in their homes. They also m
with basic computer terminology than younger atten
however, is one of unfamiliarity with rather than a lack of a
newer technology.

A class of seniors will differ from general introducto
some of your participants may have particular difficulty usir
to arthritis or other physical conditions, or they may have
web sites on a monitor with the type set at the default size. S
how to increase the default font size in the browser so th
option to do so themselves on later visits, although keep in i
ing the font size may distort the appearance of certain web
that the brightness and contrast settings on your monitors a
able levels, and familiarize yourself with the different monito
your class so that you are not fumbling with settings during

If your institution has a large number of Internet stations
public, you might consider permanently designating one or
having a larger default font size. Also invest in some 17" or
which have become much more affordable than they we
Relatively minor adjustments such as investing in a larger scr
the font size will make your computers more accessible not
but to any patron with a vision problem.

When creating handouts for your seniors-only Intern
remember the importance of readability. Use large, clear, d
plenty of white space; and always err on the side of legibility.
ally be helpful to keep in mind as you create handouts or chea
class—cluttered or fuzzy handouts will be of little use to any
the principle of readability in the forefront as you choose sites
during an Internet class for seniors. Eschew sites where desi
"cool" through the excessive use of animation, nontraditio
cramming a large amount of text and graphics together on o

Given the usual descriptions of the Internet in the media,
working under the misconception that they will encounte
pornography, viruses, and privacy theft online or that the Int
nothing to offer them. Internet training sessions offer you tl
to combat these misconceptions. During a class, demonst
designed specifically for seniors, such as Access America for Se
www.seniors.gov), Elderhostel (http://www.elderhostel.or
Senior Network (http://www.theseniornetwork.com) and reso
benefit any group, such as sites devoted to travel, health, hobbi
or investment information.

E-mail is the top reason for computer use among seniors.
especially interested in using free e-mail services to keep in tou
members and friends. Since families today tend to move arou
ever before, seniors will appreciate the ability to communicate
and grandchildren online, to post and view family photograph
in contact with their friends and relatives. Expose seniors to t
potential as a communications medium. Demonstrate free e-m
as Hotmail or Yahoo! mail, and explain the difference betwe
address and a web site address—which often can be confusing to

Technology page at http://www.aarp.org/comptech. AARP's site includes in its offerings both a learning section with tips and tutorials and hardware and software reviews for those seniors considering purchasing a PC for their home.

Especially if your library provides other programming for seniors or has a large senior population, you may want to contact ALA's Office for Literacy and Outreach Services. This office has several committees and forums focusing on how libraries can better serve seniors. Find brief descriptions of and contact information for such committees at its Services to Elderly People web site at http://www.ala.org/olos/resources/elderly.html. One additional article that will be helpful is Jeanne Holba Puacz and Chris Bradfield, "Surf's up for Seniors! Introducing Older Patrons to the Web," *Computers in Libraries* 20, no. 8 (Sept. 2000): 50–3. The authors describe their experiences in creating and refining an Internet training program for seniors at their library.

PLANNING CLASSES FOR SPECIAL GROUPS

The previous descriptions should assist you in planning classes for specific groups in your own library's service area. Any such classes you intend to offer will most likely have been thought of and previously planned out at another institution, so ask for ideas from your fellow librarians and Internet trainers. Visit nearby libraries and observe their classes; post on electronic discussion lists such as NETTRAIN, BI-L, or topical lists like REFORMA's; and network with others at library conferences and workshops.[2]

Remember, when training trainers to teach classes to specific groups, to address not only that group's particular needs but to allow time for and give guidance in locating applicable on- and offline resources for class sessions. Like any classes, Internet sessions for particular groups will be most successful when addressing their participants' interests with topical examples.

Use your creativity and your experience with your own community while planning classes to introduce all groups to the world of online communication.

NOTES

1. See the summary National Telecommunications and Information Administration (NTIA) fact sheet, "Hispanics Falling Back in Information Age" (Washington, D.C.: U.S. Dept. of Commerce, NTIA: 1999). Available: http://www.ntia.doc.gov/ntihome/digitaldivide/factsheets/hispanics.htm.

2. BI-L is an electronic discussion list for librarians interested in bibliographic instruction and user education. To subscribe, send an e-mail message to listserv@byu.edu. In the body of the message, type: sub bi-l (insert your first and last name).

5

Beyond the Basic Topics

Your library may decide that it wants to offer its community more class opportunities than just that of the basic Internet training session. Topical classes can explore the wide variety of online resources available as well as strategies for accessing and evaluating such resources. As with any Internet classes, do not underestimate the importance of making these sessions relevant to the needs and interests of your patrons. Many libraries find classes on specific topics less well-attended than basic Internet training sessions. Such programs, though, can be highly successful if you hit upon the right subject and make it relevant to your community.

Regularly offering topical classes also helps your Internet program stay fresh and shows your community that the library is innovative in creating new programs. Newer users may not automatically think to use the web to research their family's genealogy or to look for jobs, for example, or they may not be aware that the library subscribes to a variety of web-based databases such as magazine indexes or encyclopedias. Topical classes can get students thinking in new ways and provide them with the background for further online exploration on their own.

Elicit feedback from participants in your introductory Internet classes as to topics they would like to see addressed in more-advanced sessions. A common mistake of libraries offering topical programs is to choose to include only subjects they think their patrons *should* be interested in rather than topics patrons actually *want* to see covered. Give patrons a reason to attend another class by making sessions relevant to their needs. Pay attention also to your circulation statistics; if you know what types of books have been popular with your patrons, you may be able to present classes that demonstrate Internet resources on similar topics.

Create classes centered around exploring major online resources in a given topic area. As part of such classes, it may be helpful to include some discussion of the library's other types of resources on that subject as well. In a job-hunting Internet workshop, for example, you can also highlight books and software on résumé writing in addition to web-based resources. In a genealogy session, trainers can show participants the library's collection of genealogy address books, books focused on conducting a genealogical search in your state or area, and the basic use of family tree software (if available). Topical classes are a wonderful way to get people thinking about the variety of material your library has to offer in all formats.

Other topical class ideas can focus on improving participants' understanding of specific aspects of Internet use, such as web-based e-mail or online searching. Libraries should make completion of an Internet basics class (or previous familiarity with the basic use of the Internet) a prerequisite for any of these sessions. This will help to minimize disruptions by participants who might otherwise be getting in over their heads. If an unprepared student interrupts the class with questions about basic Internet use, offer to help him or her privately after the session. Allowing such students to hold up a topical session with basic how-to issues will be unfair to the other participants.

Many topical classes will be more appropriate to present as demonstrations rather than as hands-on sessions. Although hands-on practice is necessary when students are beginning to learn the medium, topical demonstrations can be presented as a way for patrons who are already familiar with the basic use of the Internet to expand their knowledge of the sort of material that is available online. In any subject-specific class, be sure to provide handouts listing and annotating every URL that will be visited during the session.

This chapter includes ideas for creating topical classes centering on the popular subjects of web-based e-mail, job hunting, and genealogy. It then goes on to provide descriptions of and tips for developing classes in topic areas that will help your patrons make better use of Internet resources: resource evaluation, Internet searching, and electronic information literacy. These ideas are merely examples of the types of classes that can be offered—think of others that may fit your community's interests, such as classes on college information online or an introduction to HTML. No library should feel compelled to use all of these ideas or even to expand beyond providing basic Internet instruction if it lacks the staff or funding for additional classes. Topical sessions can also be scheduled occasionally as tie-ins to relevant special events or as part of a larger program in the same way as can classes for particular groups.

USING FREE E-MAIL

Although most libraries do not provide users of their public Internet access terminals with personal e-mail accounts, free web-based options abound. E-mail has long been described as being the "killer application" of the Internet, and the ease of near-instantaneous and free communication can be a powerful attraction for any level of Internet user. Since around 80 percent of those using the Internet use it to send e-mail messages, large numbers of your library's public Internet users may be coming in largely, or even entirely, to check for messages and send e-mail. Patrons who are unsure of how to sign up for and use a free e-mail service will welcome the opportunity to learn.

E-mail will be a helpful class to offer as a prerequisite or suggested precursor to other topical classes. For most patrons trying to find a job online, for example, it will be necessary to create an account and to learn how to use web-based e-mail to communicate with companies and recruiters. E-mail is the most basic way for your patrons to take advantage of the Internet as an interactive medium.

Designing a Class

Consider offering a course on the uses of free e-mail services such as Hotmail, Yahoo! mail, or Mailcity. Instruction on the use of web-based e-mail can include a description of the format of an e-mail address as well as demonstrations of the process of applying for an account and choosing a user name, reading and composing messages, and sending and receiving file attachments. Make it very clear that the library is not affiliated with and does not endorse any of the free e-mail sites you mention during a class. This is crucial in part because such free web-based accounts are prone to attracting "spam," or junk e-mail.

Be sure to explain how the format of an e-mail address differs from the format of a web site address and how to tell the difference between the two. No matter how obvious this may seem to you, it will be unclear to newer Internet users. Internet beginners often try to type an e-mail address straight into the location bar of the browser or to type a web address into the To: line of an e-mail message. Include a handout such as the one on e-mail in appendix B describing the format of both types of addresses.

The first step in an e-mail class is to go through the process of applying for a free e-mail account online. Select a major service to use in your demonstration, and always have another service in mind to use as backup in case your first site is down or not responding. Demonstrate to class participants the process of filling out a web-based application form. Stress the importance of writing down their e-mail user name and password so that they can get back into their own account at a later date. Show them also how such popular services will require some creativity in choosing a user name, since many choices will already be taken.

Your next step will be to use your newly acquired account to compose an e-mail message. Sending a message to yourself at the account you just created (or to a previously created account) will allow you to demonstrate the process of sending and receiving e-mail. Show how putting your own address into the "To:" line allows you to compose a message to yourself, and then explain the use of the other elements of an e-mail message, such as the subject line, the cc: line, and the body of the message.

Once you have sent yourself a message, go back into the account's in box and show how to retrieve and read that e-mail. Explain how messages sometimes travel nearly instantaneously and sometimes get stuck in transit. A comparison to the United States Postal Service may help.

After demonstrating basic e-mail use, teach your participants how to use file attachments to send such items as digital photographs or word-processed résumés through e-mail. Have an example handy to send. Digital photos work particularly well, since services such as Hotmail display received images within the body of a message and participants can easily see how their photograph has been transmitted and received intact.

During a class, also show some ways to use e-mail to communicate with family members and friends, companies, and the library. Giving out your own e-mail address and inviting comments from students can be an innovative way of eliciting feedback from class participants without having them fill out a formal evaluation sheet. If you are teaching e-mail as a hands-on exercise, allow some time at the end of the class for all participants to practice their new skills by sending a message to your e-mail address. Trainers can also remain available in this way to answer students' additional questions long after a class session ends. If your library offers an e-mail reference service, you can promote this service during your class as well.

Discuss also how automatic "mailto:" links on web pages will not work well with free web-based e-mail services. Such links assume that a browser has a separate account and is using e-mail software such as Microsoft Outlook or Netscape Messenger. Since your students will often want to respond to items they read on a company's or individual's web site, show them how to display an actual e-mail address by pausing the mouse pointer over an e-mail link on the web. The e-mail address will show up in the bottom left hand corner of the screen, and they can then write that address down to use when composing a message in Hotmail or another free e-mail service.

Last, you may want to touch upon the subject of e-mail etiquette. Explain that unsolicited commercial e-mail (or "spam") is generally considered inappropriate by the Internet community and that it is prohibited by major free e-mail providers. Explain that a free e-mail account will attract such spam, and how to delete it unread. Also discuss the importance of being professional when using e-mail to communicate with potential employers or for other official purposes.

Resources

Most resources that discuss e-mail use focus on the functions of particular software or on the use of e-mail as a business marketing tool. However, you might want to include on your Internet shelf or in your circulating stacks some books that discuss subjects such as e-mail etiquette and how to write effective e-mail messages. The Tulsa City–County (Oklahoma) Library provides a brief instructional page on Getting Started with E-mail at http://www.tulsalibrary.org/training/tips/email.htm. Its page also includes a list of links to free web-based e-mail services.

JOB HUNTING

One of the most common uses of the Internet is in the job search, and on- and offline resources in this area abound. Libraries offering training sessions on using the Internet for job hunting have generally had a good turnout, and the high availability of material on online job searching makes planning such a class a fairly straightforward process. Job searching is also an area where patrons can see concrete results. Job seekers who watch a simple online search turn up a list of applicable positions will quickly become advocates for the presence of the Internet in the library.

Studies also show that unemployed individuals without Internet access at home are almost three times more likely to use the Internet at a public library than the national average. Nearly 22 percent of unemployed people accessing the Internet at alternative access points (other than home, school, or work) use their public library.[1] Sessions on how to use the Internet in a job search will be especially helpful to such individuals.

Designing a Class

Job hunting on the Internet is one class that can be approached in more of a "task-based" manner. Think about what participants need to know to search and apply for jobs online. In addition to having a basic familiarity with the use of the browser software, they need to be able to accomplish tasks such as the following:

> fill out online forms
>
> use a job-search engine
>
> complete a résumé on a PC and save it as text
>
> copy and paste text from a résumé or other file
>   into an online form
>
> use web-based e-mail
>
> locate companies' web sites and use them to find
>   information on a particular business

After you have identified the tasks an Internet job-seeker needs to complete, you can then focus your training sessions and handouts on teaching these tasks.

A training session can encompass the entire job search process. Start by demonstrating sites where your patrons can locate position openings online. These sites can include classified advertisement pages from your local and neighboring papers, job pages at individual companies, and large career portals such as Monster.com. Demonstrate to job seekers that they no longer have to wait for the Sunday paper to arrive so that they can sit and pore over the classifieds with a magnifying glass; they can target their employment search online and see new openings as soon as they are posted. Also discuss how keyword searching means that they no longer have to try to guess under which category a relevant job might be listed. Show how to use online forms at such career sites to limit a job search by keyword, by specific location, and by date posted.

Any training session on online job searching then needs to address formatting a résumé for the electronic environment. Demonstrate to attendees how their résumé will look when it is formatted in a program such as Microsoft Word and how it looks when it is received in plain ASCII text format through e-mail or a web-based form. (It will be helpful here to provide a handout showing the difference between the two formats. See the examples provided in appendix B.) Discuss the difference between submitting a résumé through a form or in the body of an e-mail message and attaching it to that e-mail message in word processor format. Show students how formatting such as italics, underlining, and centering are all lost and how to be creative in formatting with ASCII-only characters.

This will also be a good point to mention web-based e-mail. If your library offers a separate introductory e-mail class, you should suggest that attendees sign up. Libraries that have limited time available for teaching job searching may even want to make completion of an introduction to e-mail session or previous familiarity with web-based e-mail a prerequisite for a job searching class. During a job searching seminar, however, it will be appropriate to briefly demonstrate free e-mail services such as Hotmail. The trainer should set up his or her own web-based account before the class and demonstrate both how to compose an appropriately professional e-mail message to a potential employer and how to attach a word processor résumé file to an e-mail. Stress the importance of ensuring that the receiver of that message be able to decode the résumé, and show that many online job ads specify the format in which the company prefers to receive résumés.

After you have discussed how to attach a résumé to e-mail, also show participants how they can post their own résumés online in career databases for employers to peruse. Be sure to point out that many of these databases include the option to keep a résumé confidential in case participants are concerned about current employers finding out that they are job hunting. Be sure to demonstrate to attendees how to copy and paste text from their résumé file into a web-based form or e-mail message. Otherwise, they may assume that they need to retype their résumé information into each separate form or message.

The last portion of your session should concentrate on how participants can prepare for an interview by researching their potential employer online. Many companies have web sites detailing all sorts of corporate information, from their mission to their financial details to their corporate structure. Point out to your participants that applying for a job and researching a company online will demonstrate to potential employers that the job seekers have current, marketable skills and that learning about a company before the interview allows them the opportunity to dazzle an interviewer with their preparedness.

Monster.com and similar large sites will serve as a starting point for your participants to find career and interview advice online. If time permits, you may demonstrate some other resources in this area—many career columnists are now syndicated online, for example. Other sites that are appropriate for a class on online job hunting include those providing relocation calculators and salary survey information and those of various professional organizations (if job seekers in your class mention specific professions).

Resources

Job searching is one category that has spawned a huge number of books, articles, and web sites. In your class, plan to demonstrate the features of several major employment sites, such as Monster.com (http://www.monster.com) and Careerpath (http://www.careerpath.com). You can also mention some more-focused web pages that address the employment needs of specific groups or those in particular occupations, as well as major directories of employment resources and job sites such as The Riley Guide (http://www. dbm. com/jobguide).

Your Internet shelf and circulating stacks would benefit from the inclusion of some titles on online job searching. Some useful titles include Margaret Riley-Dikel, *The Guide to Internet Job Searching* (Lincolnwood, Ill.: VGM Career Horizons, yearly); Pam Dixon, *Job Searching Online for Dummies* (Foster City, Calif.: IDG Books, 2000); and Richard Bolles, *Job-Hunting on the Internet* (Berkeley, Calif.: Ten Speed, 1999).

Find some startling statistics on the percentage of companies that are advertising their position openings online. The ease and immediacy of posting positions on the Internet as well as the ability to attract a larger pool of candidates is encouraging more and more companies to turn to the web as a recruitment tool.

GENEALOGY RESEARCH

Genealogy is one area in which you will ideally be able to select trainers who are themselves passionate about the subject. Contact your local genealogical society, and see if it would be interested in cosponsoring a presentation on genealogical online resources at the library or if it has a person who would be willing to give such a program. Local genealogical societies are also a perfect place to advertise online genealogical training sessions or demonstrations.

Genealogy is one of the fastest growing hobbies around, and providing an introduction to online genealogical resources will help attract enthusiasts to your library. The popularity of genealogy also means that there is no shortage of online resources in this area.

Designing a Class

The specific format of a class on online genealogical resources will depend largely on your audience. When giving a demonstration to your local genealogy society, for example, you can focus less on sites that describe the process of beginning a genealogical search than if you are doing a hands-on course for genealogy beginners. Each type of class, however, can include demonstration of genealogical directories and of sites of local interest. Be sure to explain to either type of group that not all records and resources are available online and that they will not all be available online in the foreseeable future. Online information often will just give genealogists a starting place for further research or give direction to their offline activities.

A training session for genealogy beginners can begin with a demonstration of online beginners' guides. Such sites show, for example, how to start an online genealogical search, what types of records are accessible, and how to create a pedigree chart or family tree. (A variety of printable forms for genealogical record keeping are available at PBS Online's Discovering Your

Ancestors site at http://www.pbs.org/kbyu/ancestors/teachersguide/charts-records.html.)

Then demonstrate how to locate information to fill in some of the blanks on those genealogical forms. This will be an appropriate point to show a class some of the surname search engines available online and to outline the types of records that can sometimes be located on the web. Use students' own family names as examples during a class. This will help keep them interested and encourage them to participate in the session.

A genealogy for beginners session should always mention the offline resources that are available in the library. Although information on starting a search into one's family history is available online, it is not yet a substitute for the entire books that have been written on the subject. Have such books available for participants to check out after a class.

In a demonstration session for a local genealogical society or for genealogy buffs, omit descriptions of sites for beginners and get right to the meat of finding genealogical information online. Familiarize yourself with large directories such as Cyndi's List (described in the Resources section), and elicit input from participants about the types of information they are seeking. Show how to use such a directory to get to resources in specific areas.

The main difficulty with creating any class on online genealogical resources will be choosing specific sites to highlight. Genealogical material on the Internet abounds, as both amateur and professional genealogists have taken to the medium as an unprecedented way to share and locate information. In any class on genealogical resources, therefore, mention some major directories so that participants can later focus their own search on the specialized topics of their own interest.

In addition to discussing major genealogical sites, be sure to devote some time to resources of interest to local genealogists. These will include sites produced by local genealogical societies as well as sites in your state, municipality, and county where your class participants can find archival information and instructions on where to write for vital records.

Last, show participants how to use major online address directories to locate people's phone numbers and addresses nationwide. Genealogy enthusiasts are often searching for distant family members or for lost branches of their family tree, and tools such as these can save them a great deal of time and money.

Resources

The largest online genealogical directory is Cyndi's List (http://www.cyndislist.com), which you will want to demonstrate to your participants as a good starting point for their search. Cyndi's List is maintained by Cyndi Howells, who has also written the book *Cyndi's List: A Comprehensive List of 40,000 Genealogy Sites on the Internet* (Baltimore: Genealogical Publishing, 1999). This will be a good addition to the reference materials on your Internet shelf. Also consider for inclusion on your Internet shelf Elizabeth Powell Crowe's *Genealogy Online* (New York: McGraw-Hill, 1999), which contains another large list of annotated online resources for genealogists.

Out of the plethora of online genealogical resources, be sure to examine and mention the Church of Jesus Christ of Latter-Day Saints' FamilySearch (http://www.familysearch.org), which searches the International Genealogical Index, Ancestral file, and a variety of web sites for your ancestors' names. Other major sites include RootsWeb (http://www.rootsweb.com) and Family Tree Maker (http://www.familytreemaker.com), which also produces the popular software product of the same name.

Australia's Infosentials Internet Training Institute provides on its web site an example of materials it uses in teaching a genealogy resources on the Internet course. Although many of the examples it provides are specific to Australia, libraries can examine its course outline and materials as an example of the sort of information that can be taught in an introductory class. Visit its site at http://iti.infosentials.com and click on "Genealogy Course" on the right-hand side.

INTERNET SEARCH STRATEGIES

To a beginner (and even to an Internet junkie), searching for specific information on the web is often like looking for a needle in a haystack. A class on Internet search strategies can help participants develop more targeted searches, find a variety of places to start a search, and separate the useful sites from a long list of irrelevant results. Such a class can be helpful in reducing patrons' frustration in attempting to use the Internet as a research tool. You may consider targeting an Internet searching class to K–12 or college students, if your library has a large student population in its service area.

Internet searching is one class that may be more or less popular, depending on your community. Realize at the outset that it may be difficult to attract patrons to such a class, and be prepared to sell the idea to your community through advertising and through pushing this training session during other classes. Patrons who are comfortable surfing through the Internet by clicking on links and following topics of interest may not realize that they have not yet developed the searching skills necessary for more serious and focused research. Create complementary material and post it on your library's web site or make handouts available near public Internet terminals so that patrons can pursue the issue on their own.

Designing a Class

In your library's Internet basics class, you may have shown participants how to do a simple online search by using Netscape's "Search" button or a straightforward web directory such as Yahoo. Your searching strategies class will give you the opportunity to introduce your trainees to a variety of search engines and directories and to explain how to select a starting point for their online research. In addition to visiting popular sites such as Google, Yahoo, and AltaVista, also demonstrate the use of librarian-created selective directories such as the Librarians' Index to the Internet (http://www.lii.org).

Begin by describing the difference between a search engine and a web directory (or "subject index"). Although the line between the two is becoming increasingly blurred, it is still a useful distinction. Demonstrate a major directory such as Yahoo, and contrast it with a search engine such as Google. Use Yahoo's menus to drill down to resources on a desired topic, and then use Google to search for resources on the same topic. It will be helpful to try to find the same bit of information using different tools. Get students' suggestions on topics to search for; this will help to maintain their interest in the class. You can show how directories are better for locating some types of information while emphasizing that the use of search engines will be necessary in many cases.

Show how a search for the same words gives different results in each search engine. Class participants may be under the misconception that there is "one way" to search the Internet and that all information is easily and clearly available. You will be able to disabuse them of this notion quickly through such a demonstration. Explain that there is no one way to search the Internet and that there is no master directory. Visiting some of the pages that result from your initial searches will allow you to point out the nature of the Internet as a decentralized medium where anyone can publish anything.

While presenting different search engines, discuss how each of your targeted search engines has its own method of "advanced" searching. AltaVista, for example, uses a + sign to denote a term that must be included in a page for it to come up in search results, while Hotbot uses a drop-down menu in which searchers can select "all the words" to insist that all terms be included on a page. Create a handout outlining such differences between search sites. Be sure to revisit search engines and update your handouts frequently because these sites have a habit of changing their indexing strategies, format, and interface.

If your library has a web site, consider creating a section devoted to online searching with links to the resources you will demonstrate during your class. You might also want to post on your site a brief (and jargon-light) guide to Boolean searching or other helpful hints for using specific search tools. The most helpful hint you can include, however, is a note to Internet users to make their searches as specific as possible. Tell them to type in exactly what they are looking for. Internet beginners often will enter just one word into a search engine ("cats," for example, or "airplanes") when they are really looking for a very specific piece of information. Tell your participants to make their searches as explicit as possible—to search for World War II German fighter planes rather than simply for airplanes. Show how being explicit can help narrow down a search into a much more manageable and relevant set of results.

Demonstrate some subject guides to Internet resources, such as those mentioned in the section on teaching genealogy classes. Stress to students that such topical, human-created guides help to filter out extraneous information and that such sites can often be a good starting point for their search. Be sure to include such major subject guides on your own web site if you have a section on recommended Internet resources. Help visitors find a good starting point for their research on popular topics such as genealogy or job searching.

Depending on the time available for your class session, you may also mention some of the "meta" search engines such as Dogpile or MetaCrawler. Show how these sites compile results from a variety of other search engines and may be useful for a quick overview of what is available on a given subject. For fun, you can also visit one of the "search voyeur" sites such as Ask Jeeves' Peek through the Keyhole at http://www.aj.com/docs/peek to see what kind of information others are currently searching for. Be sure to use a "sanitized" site of this type if you do mention it in class, however.

You can end the session with a hands-on scavenger hunt, especially if you have a computer lab at your disposal. Have students try to find answers to selected questions using the resources and strategies discussed during the class.

Resources

Colleges, schools, and independent companies have created a variety of web sites describing the use of different search engines and recommending research strategies. SearchIQ (http://www.searchiq.com) is a good starting point for finding subject-specific search engines in new areas. For your own edification, you will also want to keep an eye on Search Engine Watch (http://www.searchenginewatch.com), which provides ratings and reviews for all major search engines as well as tips on their use. Its Search Engine Math page (http://www.searchenginewatch.com/facts/math.html) is a wonderful resource to help explain more advanced searching techniques to your group without having to get deep into Boolean logic. (See figure 5.1.)

FIGURE 5.1 Search Engine Math

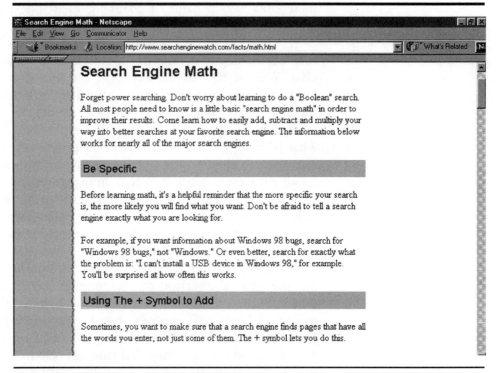

From Search Engine Watch. Copyright 2000 internet.com Corporation. All Rights Reserved. Reprinted with permission from www.searchenginewatch.com.

The University of California, Berkeley, also has a helpful Finding Information on the Internet tutorial, available online at http://www.lib. berkeley.edu/TeachingLib/Guides/Internet/FindInfo.html. Although this resource is aimed at college students and thus more thorough than may be appropriate in an introductory searching class in a public library, Internet trainers can use it as a guide in developing more succinct outlines for their own sessions.

Be sure to include on your Internet shelf and in your circulating collection books such as Reva Basch and Mary Ellen Bates, *Researching Online for Dummies* (Foster City, Calif.: IDG Books, 2000). Also take a look at Randolph Hock and Paula Berinstein, *The Extreme Searcher's Guide to Web Search Engines: A Handbook for the Serious Searcher* (Medford, N.J.: Information Today, 1999). Make sure to keep any Internet research books up to date because search engines and directories are popping up and changing constantly.

EVALUATION OF ONLINE INFORMATION

Once patrons have learned how to find information on the Internet, they will need to be able to evaluate that information before it can truly be useful to them. Knowing how to find information online is one thing; knowing how to identify useful, accurate, and relevant information online is another issue. Because the barrier to publishing material on the Internet is so low, almost anyone with an ax to grind can take a little bit of time and effort and create a professional-looking web site to present their point of view to the world.

One challenge librarians face in providing public Internet access is that the Internet is in many ways unlike any other library resource. Books, videos, and periodical articles in a library generally pass through some sort of information filter; publishers, editors, and others have validated the quality of the information and the writing. Web pages, however, face no such evaluative process. Librarians need to temper their enthusiasm for the Internet and the wealth of resources it can provide with a realistic look at the quality of much of what is out there. A class on evaluating online resources can help provide library patrons with the tools to look critically at the authority and reliability of Internet information.

Designing a Class

Create handouts with checklists that patrons can refer to when performing their own evaluations of sites that turn up in an Internet search. (An example of such a checklist can be found in appendix B.) Among the questions to ask when evaluating a site are

Who created and posted the information? Make sure that the author's name and credentials are clearly stated and that the author has some sort of authority that is specifically relevant to the information provided on the site.

Is the information accurate? Does it match information you can find in other sources? Look at the point of view or bias of the authors—are they trying to sell a product? Do they have another vested stake in your acceptance of the site's content?

Is the information current? Look for an indication of when the site was last updated.

Pick out several sites to evaluate during a class using your chosen criteria. Evaluate both authoritative, well-known sites and those that are more questionable. Choose, for instance, a site that demonstrates a clear bias. Ask participants to identify why that information may not be reliable. Then demonstrate a reputable site from a well-known source such as the Library of Congress, and show the difference in the quality of the information. Explain that anyone can put anything online—your neighbor's ten-year-old son, the Unabomber, or some bored college students with nothing better to do.

Library patrons who are new to the use of the Internet may be under the impression that information has added value merely by virtue of its being available online. This is especially true of students who will line up for computers when the answer to their question is readily available in an encyclopedia or other print source. In addition to pointing out the need to ascertain the authority of any online source, a class on resource evaluation should emphasize that not all information is available online or that it may not be available online for free.

If time permits, talk about the structure of web addresses. Point out, for example, that a ~ in a URL denotes a personal home page. Describe the difference between the top-level domains of .gov and .edu and how the information contained in such sites is often different from that contained in more familiar .com locations. Show how a domain and a web address as a whole can give a hint as to the source of a piece of information and who has created it.

A class on resource evaluation may be especially effective when targeted toward students, who, ironically, may be most reluctant to attend. Consider a cooperative effort with local school districts.

Resources

Many libraries, especially academic institutions, have created guides to assist their patrons in evaluating information they find on the Internet. One example of a detailed checklist on evaluating Internet information can be found as part of an online course sponsored by the Utah Academic Library Consortium and the Spencer S. Eccles Health Sciences Library at http://www.lib.utah.edu/navigator/Module4/eval.html. Guidelines appropriate for K–12 students can be found at Kathy Schrock's Guide for Educators—Critical Evaluation Surveys page at http://school.discovery.com/schrockguide/eval.html.

Librarians planning a course on resource evaluation should examine Hope Tillman's Evaluating Quality on the Net (http://www.tiac.net/users/hope/findqual.html), which addresses the issue of evaluating Internet sites from the library point of view. One last site to visit is Ithaca College librarian John R. Henderson's ICYouSee: T Is for Thinking at http://www.ithaca.edu/library/Training/hott.html.

ELECTRONIC INFORMATION LITERACY

As mentioned earlier, many library resources are now moving to a web-based format, and patrons who complete an introductory Internet class may appreciate an overview of your own library's subscription databases. As your library introduces a new electronic resource, you may want to schedule an initial period for staff training before the product is made available to the public so that staff can familiarize themselves with a resource before training patrons in its use (either formally or informally). Some vendors, especially if you are in a large institution/system and have made a large purchase, may provide staff training as a part of their service.

Once staff are familiar with the use of a new electronic resource, it is time to start offering training for library patrons. Patrons who are familiar with computers and with basic Internet use often will assume that they are therefore familiar with all the electronic resources the library has available. In addition to advertising the availability of your institution's electronic databases, also consider offering instructional sessions on their particular uses and features. Your courses on evaluation and searching, if provided, will address part of the information literacy equation, but you will now want to make these electronic information literacy classes specific to your library's offerings. Teach your customers skills to use when choosing where to search for information among the library's resources as well as the ability to evaluate that information.

One additional goal of information literacy is that when your patrons are able to ascertain when information may not be readily available online, they are willing to use a variety of resources to meet their research needs. Give them examples of the types of questions that can be answered by finding a book through the online catalog, through searching for magazine articles in a web-based periodicals database, and through looking in other online and print resources such as encyclopedias and almanacs. In an electronic information literacy class, your goal will be to get your participants thinking about the best resource to answer a particular informational need. Tell them straight out that not everything is on the web. Other, more specific class ideas address the use of specific web-based library resources such as the OPAC and online periodical databases.

Web-Based OPAC

Realize from the outset that many patrons may resent the very idea of having to take a class to learn how to look up a book. This is perfectly understandable! Imagine walking into the local grocery store and being told you need to take a class to find out where they keep the Cheerios. This makes as much sense on the face of it as needing to take a class to find out where the library shelves the works of John Gray or John Grisham. Some of your patrons, especially older or less-frequent library users, will prefer to avoid the OPAC altogether and will simply ask a librarian for assistance whenever they need to locate a specific item.

Regardless, your institution needs to provide its patrons with the opportunity to be trained in the use of the OPAC just as you do with any of the library's other electronic resources. Consider that your library, in the past ten to twenty years, may have gone from using a card catalog to a text- and menu-based online catalog to a web-based OPAC. Each change in format means your patrons have to figure out a new way of locating library materials. Furthermore, using web-based OPACs necessitates the use of a mouse, and the use of newer OPACs may be less intuitive for many of your patrons than even your older textual OPAC had been.

This is one class for which you will not want to make completion of Internet basics a prerequisite for attendance. Since most web-based OPACs are fairly limited in what they will allow a user to accomplish, and many libraries have security software in place to prevent OPACs from being used as Internet terminals, an OPAC course will encompass a narrowly defined set of skills. OPAC users will not need the same level of familiarity with browser functions as will regular Internet users. They may need simply to understand the use of the forward, back, and print buttons, how to type into a form, how to click on a button or link on a page, and how to scroll up and down the screen. The rest of the class can be devoted to demonstrating the features of your particular OPAC software.

In an OPAC class, show how online searching improves the way that patrons can locate needed materials. Most web-based catalogs, for example, allow users to limit their search easily by publication date, by type of material, and by language. Also demonstrate how keyword searching can be helpful when a patron is unsure of the exact title of a particular book or how to do a subject search.

If your OPAC software has special features such as the availability of PIN numbers that allow patrons to access their account information and reserve materials online, show how these capabilities can empower patrons. Become an advocate for the web-based OPAC and its enhanced capabilities. Showing patrons such interesting "extras" can help reduce any resentment they might feel at having to learn another new system.

Web-Based Periodical Databases

Patrons who are initially reluctant to give up using such familiar tools as *The Readers' Guide to Periodical Literature* may become enthusiastic converts to the new medium once they realize the sheer volume of full-text articles available in many online magazine databases. Libraries offering such services often find that their users are in fact no longer interested in any resources that do not give them instantaneous access to full text. During a class on the use of a full-text periodical database, be sure to explain to participants how to see if a particular article is available online and how to read, print, and e-mail an article to a specific address.

If your library uses a service such as InfoTrac, which includes separate databases for general, health, and business resources, start your class by explaining how to choose a database to search. This will also be important if your institution subscribes to periodical databases from different vendors or those that are centered on specific topics. Make it very clear what types of information can be found in each.

Classes on the use of periodical databases are another example of topical sessions for which libraries will not want to make previous Internet familiarity a prerequisite. Again, the use of such a database does not require previous knowledge of the use of the browser, and the few basic functions that are necessary can be taught during the session itself. Some institutions offering such training sessions, however, require that their attendees come in with basic mouse and keyboarding skills. Doing so will help a class move forward, yet those requirements will prevent many patrons from receiving instruction. This will be a larger issue if your library does not provide introductory computer training that includes the teaching of such skills.

Resources

Take a look at ALA's information literacy standards for student learning, available online at http://www.ala.org/aasl/ip_nine.html. Although they are aimed particularly at students, these standards are applicable to public library patrons as well. Another useful resource is Donald Barclay, *Teaching Electronic Information Literacy: A How-to-Do-It Manual for Librarians* (New York: Neal-Schuman, 1995), although the examples are becoming somewhat dated. Finally, the National Forum on Information Literacy maintains a web site at http://www.infolit.org. The site includes sample lesson plans, definitions, and links to other information literacy web sites.

NOTE

1. See United States Department of Commerce National Communications and Information Administration (NTIA), "Falling through the Net: Defining the Digital Divide, Part II-B" (Washington, D.C.: NTIA, 1999). Available: http://www.ntia.doc.gov/ntiahome/ fttn99/part2.html#b. The same study also notes that those using the Internet away from home are more likely to be using it in a job search than the national average.

6 Successful and Innovative Training Program Ideas

There are as many different ways to conduct a successful public Internet training program as there are libraries, but one way to ensure success is to learn from the example of others. Many libraries now offer a variety of Internet and other computer training sessions to their patrons, and most librarians and trainers are happy to share tips, training materials, sample handouts, and expertise with their fellow Internet trainers in other libraries.

This chapter presents a variety of examples of successful and innovative public Internet training programs from all sorts of libraries. Use them to glean ideas for your own library's plans, and beyond this book, remember the importance of networking with your colleagues. So many libraries now have thriving and long-running Internet training programs that there is no need for you to reinvent the wheel. Contact nearby libraries, ask for assistance on electronic discussion lists, or work through your library system to find relevant ideas and examples.

Some of the programs described here, such as fee-based classes or volunteer programs, may be more or less appropriate in different libraries' communities. Use these descriptions as examples of how to be innovative in creating your own program. As always, adapt any ideas to your institution's particular location, budget, and circumstances.

The chapter concludes with brief discussions of how to obtain grant opportunities and of working with local community groups to develop or cosponsor Internet classes.

VOLUNTEER-BASED INTERNET TRAINING PROGRAMS

Libraries and library systems that lack sufficient staff or expertise to provide Internet and computer classes to meet public demand can turn to volunteer trainers to fill that gap. Do not make the mistake of picturing the use of volunteers, however, as some magic way to create a no-cost, no-effort training program. Any successful volunteer program requires a great deal of coordination, volunteer training, recruitment, and evaluation. This is especially true when it comes to coordinating and preparing volunteers to provide public Internet training. Any computer training requires a combination of technical, training, and people skills that your potential volunteers may not initially possess.

Setting up the Volunteer Program

Setting up a volunteer technology training program will be simpler if your library has a network of volunteers already in place. If you have an existing volunteer program that you want to expand to include technology training, however, make sure that your volunteer coordinators are themselves comfortable with technology and cognizant of the skills needed by technology trainers. The use of volunteers with some existing expertise in this area will only enrich your Internet training program.

All volunteer trainers will themselves need some initial training, however. Just as it is irresponsible to throw librarians into the role of Internet trainer without any training or preparation of their own, it is even more so to expect community volunteers to step automatically into a trainer position. While volunteers may come in with the *desire* to teach, libraries need to supply them with the training and materials necessary for them to provide a consistent and effective training experience to patrons. Libraries using volunteers to conduct Internet training sessions must hold them to the same standard of professionalism and effectiveness during those sessions as they would staff trainers. Your volunteers will be acting as representatives of the library while teaching library patrons. Patrons will not necessarily make the distinction between staff and volunteer trainers and are entitled to the same level of service in each class.

Make computer and Internet skills a prerequisite for volunteers. In this way, training classes for volunteer trainers can focus specifically on teaching and presentation skills as well as on the importance and content of the curriculum you want transmitted to the public. Some libraries advertising for volunteer trainers have been inundated with responses from novice computer users who misunderstood the offer of train-the-trainer sessions as an opportunity to themselves be taught Internet and computer skills—so make any promotional materials extremely clear as to the library's expectations of potential trainers. Consider screening volunteer candidates for suitability before devoting staff time and resources to training them. Try advertising for volunteers on your library's web page so that candidates will have to possess some Internet expertise just to run across the announcement.

If potential volunteers turn out to be technologically savvy yet lacking in the qualities necessary for a good trainer, ensure that you have other options in mind. Try not to tell a volunteer that you will be unable to use their skills; instead, point them toward setting up and maintaining machines, loading software, or creating publicity materials and handouts. Show them that their efforts are appreciated in whatever capacity.

When considering creating a volunteer program, also keep in mind the need to reassure existing staff that their jobs are secure and that the use of community volunteers in this area does not minimize the importance of staff expertise. It is important to secure the backing of library staff before initiating any such program. Point out that the use of volunteers for group training removes some extra responsibility from library staff and frees up time for librarians to pursue other professional activities and perform their own day-to-day duties more effectively.

Remember also that volunteers, no matter how skilled, cannot be relied on in the same way as can paid staff members. Beware of becoming overly reliant on just one or two volunteers to conduct Internet training, and always have a plan for offering classes if a volunteer should leave. Often the best way to accomplish this will be to use a combination of staff and volunteer trainers to conduct sessions so that there will always be another trainer ready to step in. This will also help to reassure staff that their positions are not being supplanted by volunteers.

While most libraries with large volunteer programs are relatively large districts or systems, small libraries can consider establishing a similar program on a less-elaborate scale. Small institutions may want to cooperate with other nearby libraries or with their consortium, perhaps splitting the cost of a program coordinator or trainer for volunteers. Volunteers then would be able to teach across several different libraries, or classes could be centralized at the largest or best-equipped library building in the group. If you are considering establishing such a program, learn from libraries such as the King County (Washington) Library System and D.C. Public Libraries (whose programs are described in the following sections). Require formal training of and commitment from your volunteers.

Consider a cooperative effort with the local high school district or community college. Many high schools are now requiring students to volunteer a certain number of hours of community service as a prerequisite for graduation, and Internet-savvy teenagers may surprise you with their abilities and enthusiasm. You may not want to have high school students teaching formal classes, and you will have to be very careful in choosing the teen volunteers and training them. The efforts of local teenagers, however, can help supplement formal training sessions. Teens can be especially effective in providing one-on-one help on a walk-in basis to patrons who are struggling at an Internet terminal or online catalog. They can also serve as computer lab monitors, helping free up librarians to teach formal training classes or to pursue other professional duties.

Cooperating with the school will provide an additional check, as you can work with teachers to help select teenagers with technical skills, people skills, and patience. These teens will have the added incentive of knowing that their best efforts are necessary to gain community service credit.

On the other end of the volunteer spectrum, look to retirees who want to keep up with their technical skills while getting the opportunity to interact with others. Retirees may be especially effective as trainers for senior-only classes (as described in chapter 4). You also may look to volunteers to serve as translators for non-English-speaking patrons.

The King County (Washington) Library System's Netmaster Program

Any library considering creating a training program using volunteer trainers would benefit from examining established volunteer programs such as that at Washington State's King County Library System (KCLS). KCLS has been running a volunteer trainer (Netmaster) program since late 1996. Public Internet, introduction to computers, and Microsoft Office classes throughout the system are taught by a combination of staff and volunteer trainers. Details of the program and instructions for Netmaster can be viewed online at http://www.jetcity.com/~skahn/netmaster-manual.html. See figure 6.1 for a brief view of the KCLS Netmaster online training materials.

KCLS provides its Netmaster trainers with very detailed information on how to conduct training classes and requires all potential volunteers to attend a hands-on training session before teaching their first public class. Since the goal is for a consistent curriculum and training experience across all KCLS libraries, each volunteer is provided with standardized training materials, handouts, a class outline, and training tips. Trainers must commit to teaching at least four public classes in exchange for the training they themselves receive at their train-the-trainer session.

The use of volunteers allows KCLS to meet the demand for Internet and other computer training classes across a forty-library system serving a population of more than one million. KCLS uses a combination of two full-time and three part-time staff trainers, interested librarians at individual branches,

FIGURE 6.1
King County (Washington) Library System's Netmaster Volunteer Training Materials

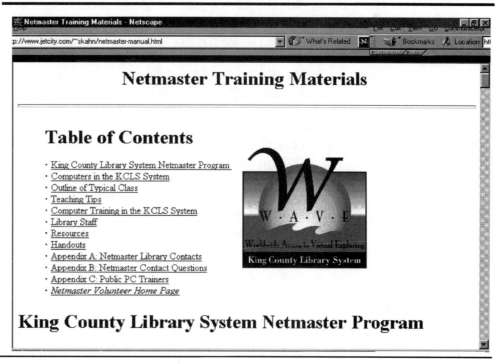

and community volunteers to teach a variety of computer training classes to the public. Each library building has a Netmaster contact who coordinates scheduling of volunteers at that particular library—after those volunteers have been trained by KCLS staff trainers. Because of the success and scope of the Netmaster program, those librarians at KCLS branch libraries who have little desire (or time) to conduct Internet training sessions are not required to teach.

The District of Columbia Public Libraries' Volunteer-Based Program

Other libraries, such as the District of Columbia Public Libraries, also use a combination of staff and volunteers to train the public. Libraries using volunteer trainers have independently created remarkably similar requirements and programs. Like KCLS, the D.C. Public Libraries, for example, also have a large pool of volunteer instructors. These instructors are required to attend a two-hour trainer orientation, to observe at least one class session before starting to teach, and to commit to teaching at least one class each month for six months. A (initially grant-funded) customer training coordinator runs the computer-training program and is responsible for recruiting volunteers. Classes have proved extremely popular; in 1999 alone, the D.C. Public Libraries provided free computer training to more than 2,500 people.

Resources

When considering the establishment of any volunteer program, especially one as complex as a technology training program, you may want to consult one of the professional manuals available for library volunteer coordinators. Such titles include Bonnie McCune and Charleszine Nelson, *Recruiting and Managing Volunteers in Libraries: A How-to-Do-It Manual for Librarians* (New York: Neal-Schuman, 1995), and Sally Gardner Reed, *Library Volunteers—Worth the Effort! A Program Manager's Guide* (Jefferson, N.C.: McFarland, 1994). These books will help you establish and manage your program and will provide arguments for the viability of using volunteers in your library. Also be sure to visit the KCLS web page mentioned previously and examine the materials it provides to its volunteers.

When creating an application process for volunteers, look at other libraries' application forms such as the one available online from Multnomah County (Oregon) Library at http://www.multnomah.lib.or.us/lib/vol/application.html. See what kind of questions it asks to help determine the suitability of volunteers for computer-related programs and for other opportunities within the library.

PAY TO PLAY

Although the notion of charging for Internet classes may be anathema to some librarians, more and more libraries are finding it necessary to impose at least a minimal fee on participants to help offset the cost of providing training. Libraries such as the Harrison County Library in Mississippi, for example, charge participants $5 per class to help defray the cost of materials. Those charging such minimal fees look upon them as a cost-recovery effort similar to that of charging for photocopies, fee-based database searches, or computer printouts. Fees also help reduce the all-too-common occurrence of patrons signing up for a class and simply not showing up, rather than canceling so that another customer could take their place.

Some libraries have gone further and turned Internet training into a money-making proposition. Their fee-based classes allow them to provide a service to their community, help them position themselves as technology leaders, and raise funds for the library at the same time. Patrons are also more likely to take for-fee classes seriously. As librarians have long ago learned, money and respect often go hand-in-hand. Additionally, if library gadflies such as Steve Coffman of Los Angeles County Public Library's FYI fee-based information service are correct, such revenue-generating services are the wave of the future and essential to the future survival of libraries themselves.[1] Libraries' expanded role as a center of technology and training may require a change in philosophy so that the costs of providing such new services do not undermine the library's ability to carry out its traditional activities.

Fees for Internet classes, however, will not be a significant revenue stream for your library. Even if your institution imposes higher fees than just the minimal charges to pay for the cost of copying handouts, it will likely merely recover the costs of developing and running the program. Also be aware that charging for Internet classes can open up some libraries to charges of unfair competition from a tax-supported body and can endanger their not-for-profit status. Furthermore, some libraries are located in states that prohibit them from charging fees for library services. Consult with your institution's attorney before initiating any such fee-based program.

The intention here is not to rehash the arguments for or against establishing fee-based Internet classes (or any fee-based service) in libraries but, rather, to provide libraries that have decided to implement such a program with the information and resources that they need to do so effectively.

Setting Up the Fee-Based Program

Charging fees for training will meet with less resistance from patrons and staff members if fees are charged from the very beginning of your Internet training program. Your library will find it much more difficult to change classes that used to be free into a fee-based service.

Before establishing a fee-based Internet training program at your library, determine whether such classes will be appropriate in your community. You will need support both from your local community and from your institution's administration. A fee-based program will be appropriate only if your library establishes that Internet training classes are a supplement to basic library services, rather than an integral part of the library's offerings. Such classes may be less controversial in your institution than more typical fee-for-information services, depending on whether training is seen as a basic library function or as such a "value-added" service.

Internet training can be seen as peripheral to the library's mission of connecting its users with information. Patron access to the information on the Internet remains free, while the library charges only for the training that can facilitate access to such information. Fee-based classes present an opportunity for your library to offer additional services while receiving the same level of funding.

Some libraries also offer a mixture of free and fee-based sessions, depending on the level of time and effort that goes into planning and conducting a particular class. As part of such a program, you can consider offering your patrons the option of attending free large-group demonstration sessions using a projector unit. These are easier to plan and teach than are hands-on workshops, and will take less time and effort on the part of trainers. The option of attending a free demonstration will satisfy a large group of patrons who just want a look at what the Internet is, yet may understandably be reluctant to pay for the privilege. In addition to such free presentations, your library can then give patrons the option of attending additional hands-on, fee-based sessions to learn and practice their skills.

In some situations charging for Internet training is inappropriate. Do not even consider charging for your Internet classes, for example, if your library lacks a computer lab. Libraries with successful fee-based training programs are generally larger institutions or systems with devoted, full-time trainers and separate hands-on teaching facilities. Furthermore, patrons will balk at being charged for sessions unless they resemble a "real" class, and small-group sessions clustered around a public terminal are just too informal to qualify. If possible, use any fees to pay a portion of the salary of a dedicated, full-time trainer or training coordinator. Libraries serving large numbers of low-income residents, likewise, should avoid charging fees for training. In this case, it may be more advantageous for a library to apply for grants to help defray the cost of providing classes than to charge for such sessions.

You will want to conduct some market research to determine whether your community's residents will be willing and able to pay fees for Internet training at the library and to help establish the level of such fees. Also create a written marketing plan to help sell your program to the community.[2] The success of your program will depend on your being able to attract customers, which may require some nontraditional selling strategies on the part of your library. Be sure to issue a press release announcing the availability and pricing structure of your classes and to devote a good amount of PR to promoting them. Collect testimonials from satisfied clients and use them in your advertising materials.

Also offer additional classes to help attract satisfied participants back to your program. Charging fees may allow your library to offer more variety in its program of training sessions. (For ideas on creating topical and diverse classes, see chapters 4 and 5.)

Choosing the level of fees to charge will be somewhat more of a challenge. There are two ways to determine an appropriate fee: Determine what is charged in the private sector and decide how closely you wish to match such programs; or attempt to calculate the cost to your library of providing classes and decide how much of that cost you wish to recover and how high the charges will need to be to do so. Look at the level of fees that other libraries such as those described in the following sections have successfully charged, and adapt their program ideas and fee schedules as appropriate for your community.

You will also need to create a written proposal for your director and library board. In the plan, outline

> what classes you intend to offer
>
> what fees you will charge
>
> who will be the targeted audience
>
> who will teach the sessions
>
> how the money will be handled and collected
>
> what fund the money will go into
>
> what revenue goals you have for the program
>
> what the goal of providing the service itself will be

Allot some funds for the planning and startup stages of creating a program of training sessions, which must be done before classes start and before any revenue is coming in from your sessions.

A related option for libraries lacking the staff, funding, or expertise to themselves provide Internet training for patrons is to partner with an outside company, letting it use your space and equipment to provide lower cost training than could otherwise be justified. In this case, be sure to make it clear in any promotional materials that such classes are provided by an outside institution and that the training is not library-created. Fees are then charged by the outside agency rather than by the library itself, although the library may collect a percentage of any fees or charge a flat fee for the use of its equipment. Libraries might also consider imposing fees for classes only on nonresidents of the library district or local community. In this case, the argument for charging fees will be that residents have already contributed toward the cost of the program through their local taxes, while nonresidents have not.

The Richmond (British Columbia) Public Library's Fee-Based Program

Few public libraries currently charge their patrons more than minimal fees to participate in public Internet classes. The Richmond Public Library (RPL) in British Columbia, Canada, however, has trained thousands of people to use the Internet with a combination of free and fee-based programs.[3] All RPL librarians are required to teach computer training sessions, and both teaching and computer skills are basic requirements for entry-level candidates. Because of RPL's commitment to technology and teaching, all entry-level librarian candidates are now required to complete technological proficiency and aptitude tests as well as to demonstrate their ability to teach computer subjects.

RPL customers have the option of signing up for a free introduction to the Internet class, which is a demonstration-only session held for audiences averaging about fifty people per class. These classes are "live" demonstrations rather than PowerPoint presentations, and they use audience suggestions to keep sessions interactive and to demonstrate sites on topics in which audience members are interested. The library does, however, charge a fee for all hands-on training sessions, including basic hands-on Internet, classes for seniors, and topical sessions such as Internet for parent and child and Internet searching for people in business. Figure 6.2 shows the home page for the hands-on Internet classes offered at RPL.

RPL conducted a market study to determine the appropriate fees for its hands-on sessions, and it currently charges $59 (Canadian) per person or $65 per couple (sharing one computer) for each 2½-hour class. The library offers senior-only training sessions at a discounted rate of $15. Mouse and keyboarding skills are a prerequisite for all hands-on classes, which are taught in smaller 15-to-20-person sessions in separate computer labs. A partnership with the local paper ensures that the library's class schedule is published and that classes and other library services remain in the public eye.

FIGURE 6.2
Richmond (British Columbia) Public Library's Fee-based Hands-on Internet Classes

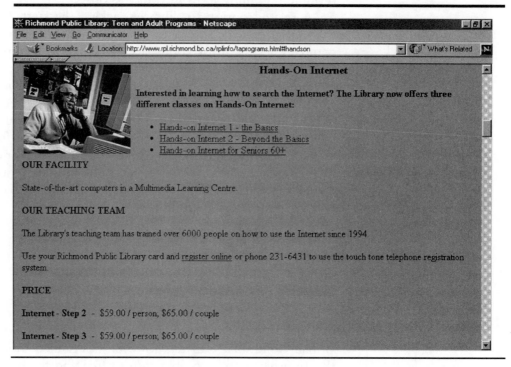

The Vancouver (British Columbia) Public Library's Fee-Based Program

The Vancouver Public Library (VPL), in British Columbia, has a similar program to that of RPL. It offers its patrons a free 1½-hour demonstration class combining slides and live demonstration as well as for-fee hands-on sessions. Fees are also similar; VPL offers its patrons a 3½-hour Internet for beginners class for $55 (Canadian) and a 4-hour searching the Internet class for $65. Classes are limited to fifteen students each and are conducted in a separate training lab.

Resources

Any library considering establishing a fee-based public Internet training program (or other fee-based service) should take a look at Multnomah County (Oregon) Library's web site for "entrepreneurial libraries" at http://www. multnomah.lib.or.us/lib/products/entre. Your institution might also want to subscribe to the *Marketing Library Services* newsletter from Information Today. Subscription information and sample articles can be found online at http://www.infotoday.com/mls/mls.htm.

For an overview of calculating the cost of a service and creating cost-recovery programs in libraries, see Murray S. Martin and Betsy Park, *Charging and Collecting Fees and Fines: A Handbook for Libraries* (New York: Neal-Schuman, 1998). Although they do not specifically address the issue of charging fees for Internet training sessions, the authors discuss many related issues such as imposing fees for online searching or for Internet access itself. Also examine Alice Sizer Warner, *Making Money: Fees for Library Services* (New York: Neal-Schuman, 1989).

TAKING IT ON THE ROAD

Community groups such as Rotary Club, women's clubs, and senior centers are often searching for speakers on a variety of topics. Why not take your Internet training sessions on the road?

Bringing an Internet introduction to groups such as the PTA, local senior center, or school board will allow your library to reach people who may not naturally think to come to the library for Internet use. Providing introductory instructions or topical demonstrations will help your library be seen as a technology leader and may help draw new users to the library. Libraries that provide such outside training, especially those training seniors, have drawn in some participants who had not been to the library in person in years. Such classes provide a perfect opportunity to promote a library's programs, services, and collections, especially when demonstrating the resources available on your library's web page.

Setting up the Program

In many cases, it may be appropriate to provide demonstration-only presentations to outside groups. Demonstrate web sites and other online resources in the group's area of interest, and stress that hands-on practical training is available in the library. A demonstration-only session can also be appropriate when presenting to groups or institutions that already have Internet access and a basic familiarity with its use. The session can then show these groups how to use their existing skills to research topics online in their own areas of interest. It can also provide a taste of what is available online from the library and, generally, in subject-appropriate areas.

The logistics of taking enough equipment on the road and of providing connectivity to all stations may limit what libraries can provide outside their physical institution. The first step, then, will be to determine how connectivity will be established and what equipment will be used to provide training outside the library. Libraries have several major options. First, you can bring laptops or other portable equipment to your designated location and establish a dialup Internet connection once there. The connection, however, may be slow—especially when it is shared among several stations. You also need to ensure that the place where you are providing training has a telephone line that can be used for such a purpose; modem connections cannot be established through many commercial phone systems, for example.

Second, if your targeted institution currently has Internet access in place, you then may be able to either temporarily hook your own equipment into the institution's network to establish a connection for training or provide training using its computers. This may be possible in places such as senior centers or schools, for example. In locations that do not yet have Internet access in place, you might consider establishing permanent remote stations there. This will be appropriate if you have the funding and if you are intending to provide a regular program of Internet and computer instruction. Connection and equipment costs can then sometimes be shared with the institution.

Last, some libraries have been successful providing on-the-road Internet access and classes through converting former bookmobiles into "cybermobiles." Those libraries are able to establish a wireless Internet connection aboard the vehicle through a satellite or other wireless connection. Be sure to investigate all of your connectivity options thoroughly before committing to one technology, since wireless technology is constantly progressing. You will also want to pick the method that will be best for your purposes.

Cybermobiles can be brought to a variety of locations, and classes can be taught on board at regularly scheduled times and places. One drawback to this method, however, is that students have to get themselves onto the vehicle for instruction. This may be difficult for residents in assisted-living facilities and other senior residences. Also consider logistical issues such as the noise created by a generator and the space needed on-board for computer and other equipment.

Once connectivity and the training environment have been established, you must decide what types of classes will be useful to community groups in locations outside the library. You may want to provide general introductions to computers and the Internet itself, or you may want to focus on familiarizing students with electronic library resources such as the library's web page, online catalog, and magazine databases. The format and content of classes will vary depending on the specific groups you will be teaching.

Also be sure to devote sufficient time to finding and training trainers for these special outside sessions. This will be crucial if your library intends to use volunteers to conduct its on-the-road instruction. (See the beginning of this chapter for information on recruiting and using volunteer trainers.)

The Richmond (British Columbia) Public Library's on-the-Road Program

The Richmond Public Library (whose fee-based program was mentioned earlier) conducts Internet training sessions for organizations such as school boards, city staff, and community groups. RPL charges for these training sessions and can collect up to several thousands of dollars for a full-day class with a group such as a local school board.

The Multnomah County (Oregon) Library's Cyber Seniors Program

Many public libraries, however, have begun taking Internet training on the road without imposing a charge on recipients. The Multnomah County Library (MCL) in Oregon, for example, started its Cyber Seniors program in the spring of 2000. During the late 1990s the library noticed a decrease in the number of senior citizens using the library. Suspecting that this drop in usage was due to a discomfort with the library's increasing reliance on computer technology, MCL applied for a grant from its local telephone company, U.S. West, to help it bring computer and Internet instruction to local senior centers. Bringing instruction to where seniors are has proved popular, as the library had an overwhelmingly positive response from senior centers. After very minimal advertising, as many as fifty seniors signed up for the initial program at one location.

MCL has used a portion of the grant money from U.S. West to purchase eight slimline computers for use in training seniors. Specially trained volunteers bring the PCs on the road (along with one laptop for the instructor) in their cybermobile and set them up at local senior centers. They use a full-sized keyboard and mouse to get students used to using computers with a setup similar to the one they will encounter in the library. Since the grant is from the phone company, MCL has the advantage of a high-speed installed DSL (Digital Subscriber Line) connection at centers within a DSL service area. The library's grant pays for the initial DSL connection setup fee and for monthly service for as long as the senior center uses the training service. At locations without access to a DSL connection, trainers either establish a dialup Internet connection for the duration of the class or hook their training PCs into the center's existing Internet access.

Volunteers can train six seniors at a time. MCL offers four modules through this program: computer basics, Internet searching and e-mail, the online catalog, and the library's web page. These modules are taught as individual two-hour sessions, and MCL volunteers will come to the center four times for each six-person group so that seniors have an opportunity to attend each class.

MCL's existing volunteer program has given it a leg up in providing on-the-road instruction to its senior community. Initial volunteer trainers for the Cyber Seniors program came from the library's existing pool of volunteers, many of whom were already trained to help library users with the use of the Internet as well as with the library's catalog. MCL also put an ad in the local paper to attract additional volunteers. Volunteers who have not already taken the library's training for technology trainers are required to take a six-hour Technohost training class before becoming qualified to train. In such classes they learn to use the library's catalog and other databases, to use the library's web page, to troubleshoot printing problems, and to use the library's usage-monitoring software. They also receive some additional training on teaching seniors, and conduct a practice session in which they set up the actual PCs that will be used at the senior centers and go over the Cyber Senior curriculum.

The Farmington (Michigan) Community Library's CyberSeniors Program

The Farmington Community Library (FCL) in Michigan also provides a CyberSeniors program that takes Internet instruction to senior centers and to assisted-living facilities. FCL, however, takes a somewhat different approach than does MCL to establishing connectivity and to teaching classes. In 1997, FCL received an LSTA grant that the library used to purchase two PCs and printers and books on using the Internet and the browser software. It set up this material at a local senior center and at an assisted-living center and left it in place for seniors to use during and after training sessions. Each seniors institution agreed to install a phone line to establish Internet connectivity for these machines. In 2000, a corporate donation allowed FCL to add three more sites to the program, expanding Internet access and classes to nursing-home sites where residents are less mobile. At these sites, trainers provide all hands-on, individual sessions. Seniors who are able are also invited to attend Internet training sessions at the library.

The initial goal of FCL's CyberSeniors program was to teach seniors how to use the library's electronic resources. FCL chose seniors because it sees itself as a facilitator of lifelong learning and because seniors were a group that seemed to see technology passing them by. FCL's training allows seniors to become comfortable with using the Internet and with e-mail, which lets them communicate with family and friends online.

Initially, library trainers visited the nursing home weekly for three months until seniors were comfortable using the computers and accessing library resources. Trainers then recruited a volunteer in residence who carries on the program and makes sure that computers remain in working condition. Library trainers now visit the center once a month.

At the senior center, library trainers provide two-hour classes once a week that are taught by a combination of volunteers and the library's outreach staff member. They offer six sessions in regular rotation, including classes on the use of the mouse and keyboard, using the library home page, and using e-mail. Such classes include a one-hour general program in which a trainer shows a video and is available to answer questions. The trainer then provides individual hands-on training in 10-to-15-minute blocks to interested seniors. Since classes rotate, seniors are free to repeat sessions or to come in at any point during the rotation. They are also able to come back for sessions they may have missed.

Muncie (Indiana) Public Library's Cybermobile

Perhaps the most famous example of on-the-road Internet instruction is the Muncie Public Library (MPL) in Indiana's Cybermobile, which first hit the road in October 1998. (See figure 6.3.) Initially funded in part by LSTA money and by corporate contributions of software and computer equipment, this converted bookmobile offers wireless on-board Internet access through a combination of a cellular modem and a satellite connection. When an Internet connection is unavailable, the library provides classes using Internet demonstration software. In 1999, the first full year of Cybermobile service, MPL offered 142 two-hour-long computer classes on board the vehicle— around three class sessions a week. Six hundred forty-one people were trained in computer skills ranging from computer basics to Microsoft Word to Internet basics.

Through the Cybermobile, MPL provides training and access to a variety of community groups and at a number of locations. On-board classes have been provided at places such as senior centers, apartment complexes, elementary schools, community centers, and the Muncie Mission. Classes have been taught to groups as diverse as ESL students, people in community corrections, seniors, and Head Start families. The Cybermobile allows MPL to help bridge the digital divide and to bring free Internet access and training to individuals who might otherwise be left out. After each class, students are invited to visit their local library branch and are told of the other class opportunities, free computer access, and other services and materials available there.

FIGURE 6.3 Muncie (Indiana) Public Library's Cybermobile

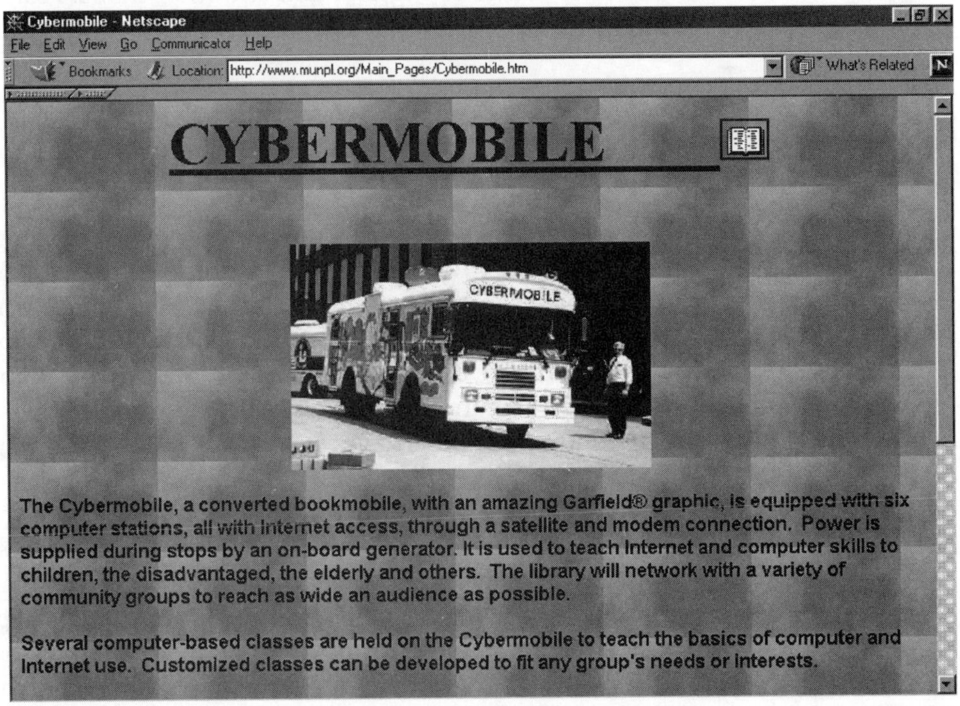

Photograph copyright the Muncie Public Library. Garfield design © PAWS.

Community groups, agencies, and businesses are invited to schedule Cybermobile stops and classes at their locations, and these can be worked out with the Cybermobile coordinator. The Cybermobile has been a great publicity opportunity for the library; it has been featured in forums as diverse as National Public Radio, an Indianapolis news station, and *Computers in Libraries*. The Cybermobile coordinator and the library's assistant director have also made personal appearances at a variety of library conferences and in front of local groups to discuss the program.

Resources

Much has been written about Muncie's Cybermobile. Any library contemplating establishing mobile Internet access should peruse such information. See, for example, the library's own web site, which includes the 1999 annual report for the vehicle at http://www.munpl.org/Main_Pages/Cybermobile_Update.htm. Also see Karen Schneider, "The Cybermobile: A Groovy Set of Wheels," *American Libraries* 29, no. 8 (Sept. 1998): 76–7, which is accessible online at http://www.ala.org/alonline/netlib/il998.html.

Aside from specific articles on the Cybermobile, little has been written for libraries seeking to take Internet instruction on the road. However, see Eric Lease Morgan, "A Different Type of Distance Education," *Computers in Libraries* 19, no. 2 (Feb. 1999): 35. This article, accessible online at http://www.infotoday.com/cilmag/feb99/story1.htm, describes two other libraries' remote Internet training programs. Also check with your local library system and with larger nearby institutions to see if any of them have established such a program, and ask other trainers for their advice.

GRANT-FUNDED INTERNET TRAINING PROGRAMS

Many libraries have created successful Internet training programs for staff and patrons through the use of grant funding. Few libraries have the resources to pay for all of the technology and services they would like to provide, and grants can be a useful way of filling in those gaps. Since a variety of applicable grants have been mentioned previously, the possibility is discussed here only briefly. Note that many of the innovative and successful programs mentioned throughout this book got their start through grant funding, helping to alleviate the costs of setting up a major Internet training program.

Always consider how your library will pay for or modify your training program when the grant money runs out. Grants will often supply just the seed money to get your program off the ground and may be more appropriate for use in providing the initial money for equipment and initial train-the-trainer training than in funding an ongoing effort. Although grant money paid to retrofit the Muncie Public Library's Cybermobile, for example, its operating costs and the coordinator's salary currently come out of the library's own operating budget.

Applying for Grant Funding

In applying for a grant, your library will need to provide detailed plans as to how the money will be spent. Examine grant-funded programs from other libraries to gain ideas for your own training; each of the programs in the section on training on the road, for instance, was initially grant-funded. Be willing to look beyond LSTA funding for grant opportunities from a variety of foundations and corporations.

The process of preparing a grant proposal will also be useful in helping you organize Internet training program plans. Even if a grant opportunity falls through, your proposal will provide you with a detailed blueprint of how your institution would ideally proceed. Scale down your plans to what you can afford, or use them to find alternate funding for your program.

If you are new at applying for grants, look at some of the many online and print resources available for detailed instructions on creating a successful proposal. To help you in writing your grant proposal and in locating additional opportunities, see the Pacific Bell Knowledge Network Explorer grants web page at http://www.kn.pacbell.com/wired/grants. It gives links to pages detailing how to submit a successful grant application, information on locating appropriate grants, and links to relevant online journals. The Foundation Center's web page also provides a proposal writing short course at http://fdncenter.org/onlib/shortcourse/prop1.html.

Resources

See the sections in the previous chapters for appropriate grant suggestions for specific types of classes. The most common source of grant money for establishing an Internet training program in public libraries is LSTA funding, which many institutions have used successfully to create innovative and long-running programs. LSTA grants are generally administered through each state library; contact your own state library for grant guidelines and information. Also check with your state library for other state or state-administered grant opportunities.

The Gates Library Initiative can also provide funding for building a computer lab, purchasing software, and training trainers. States that are currently eligible for this program as well as guidelines for applying are listed online at http://www.gatesfoundation.org/learning/libraries/libraryprogram/usguidelines.htm. ALA also provides a description of grants and printable applications at http://www.ala.org/work/awards/grants.html. This page links to additional descriptions of grants from ALA divisions and those of outside agencies.

For other grant opportunities, check with your local phone company, your state library association, and large technology companies in the area. Peruse the web sites of such institutions; sometimes they provide grants that are not specifically aimed at libraries but that may be applicable for providing funding for a technology training program. Look for foundations that have provided library funding in the past, and identify those that have made grants similar to the one you are requesting; these foundations may be more receptive to your ideas. Start online at The Foundation Center (http://fdncenter.org), which allows you to look up foundation information and to subscribe to a weekly philanthropy news e-mail newsletter.

One useful starting point for any library looking for grant opportunities is Gina-Marie Cantarella, *National Guide to Funding for Libraries and Information Services* (New York: The Foundation Center, 1999). This book contains entries for hundreds of foundations and corporate giving programs that have shown interest in funding library-related programs. Be sure to also peruse the May 2000 issue of *Computers in Libraries,* which contains articles by librarians who have successfully obtained grant money for technology and training and help in writing a grant proposal. This issue also includes fundraising ideas and other suggestions on paying for computer equipment and services. See also The Taft Group for the American Library Association, *The Big Book of Library Grant Money 1998–99* (Chicago: American Library Assn., 1998) with nearly 2,200 profiles of grants.

WORKING WITH COMMUNITY GROUPS

Another idea for libraries seeking to expand their program of Internet instruction is to work with local groups or institutions that may be willing to help sponsor or provide such programs at the library. This concept was briefly touched upon in the section on fee-based programs, although this arrangement may not always involve fees.

Internet instruction is an area in which partnership with local community groups can be very rewarding. This will be easier to accomplish if your library already has a good working relationship with local agencies, groups, and businesses. Working with community agencies may be an especially useful proposition for small institutions that have difficulty finding grant funding or whose programs are too small in scale to attract the interest of a large foundation. These smaller programs can be the right size for funding or participation by local groups and businesses. If you choose to work with other agencies, though, make sure to clearly delineate each party's contribution and responsibilities, preferably in writing. This leaves no room for later confusion.

Sponsorship

Always be on the lookout for groups that would be natural cosponsors for an Internet training program. Libraries have been successful coproducing technology training with groups ranging from their own Friends group to the local chamber of commerce. Sponsorship may be particularly helpful when it comes to bringing in an outside trainer or presenter, whether to give a special program to the community or to train librarians to themselves provide training to the public.

Be sure to give your sponsoring agency, group, or business prominent credit on all promotional materials created for the program. This is often "reward" enough for a local institution because it will appreciate the positive publicity stemming from being associated with a popular program.

Cooperation

Your library likely serves as a community meeting place and brings in a variety of speakers and presenters to provide programs for the community. Internet demonstrations are a natural addition to this community-center role. Perhaps the local genealogical society has a computer buff who would like to demonstrate genealogical resources online, or maybe the local chamber of commerce has a small ISP or computer training institute member who would like to present a program on how to get online. Advertise for speakers and presenters on Internet topics, tapping into the expertise of your local community and community groups.

Your library need not create all its Internet programs itself, just as it need not provide all of its own speakers or programs in any other area. Library communities are used to seeing the library as a public center that provides space for a variety of different programs, provided by a variety of different institutions and individuals.

Use outside resources and the other innovative ideas and examples provided in this chapter to create a useful and unique Internet training program at your own library. Open your mind to the variety of possibilities in designing successful Internet instruction. The time has come for many libraries to move beyond the basics and expand their class offerings, helping them remain relevant in the Internet era.

NOTES

1. Steve Coffman, "'And Now, a Word from Our Sponsors . . .': Alternative Funding for Libraries," *Searcher* 8, no. 1 (Jan. 2000): 51–7. Available: http://www.infotoday.com/searcher/jan00/coffman.htm. Read about the FYI program at https://fyi.co.la.ca.us.

2. For information on how to write a library marketing plan for fee-based services, see Amelia Kassel, "How to Write a Marketing Plan," *Marketing Library Services* 13, no. 5 (June 1999). Available: http://www.infotoday.com/mls/jun99/how-to.htm.

3. Internet training and the entire RPL Internet strategy are described in Cate McNeely, "Repositioning the Richmond Public Library for the Digital Age: One Library's Perspective," *Library and Information Science Research* 21, no. 3 (5 Oct. 1999): 391–406. Current free and for-fee classes are outlined on their web site at: http://www.rpl.richmond.bc.ca/rplinfo/programs.html.

7

Evaluating Your Program

The very word "evaluation" can strike terror into the heart of a beginning trainer. Yet it is important for a library to collect feedback on the style and effectiveness of its individual trainers and the content of its classes, and occasionally to undertake a thorough evaluation of the entire Internet training program. We all have blind spots and usually are most blind when it comes to our own performance. It is easy to be either overly complacent or overly negative, and collecting feedback from others will help fill in those blanks.

Without regular evaluation, you cannot know whether your training sessions are truly meeting their objectives and meeting the needs of class participants. Trainers should be encouraged to look at evaluation as an opportunity to learn and to increase the effectiveness of their classes. Reflecting and acting upon feedback from trainees, fellow trainers, or other observers will help trainers develop their skills and create classes that will meet the institution's objectives for Internet training. Evaluation will also keep trainers from becoming too comfortable with the status quo. Without feedback, it is easy to assume that sessions are proceeding well, when in fact participants may be utterly confused.

Evaluations can address both the content of Internet training sessions and the presentation or teaching style of particular trainers. Evaluation forms and informal oral evaluations should address both aspects of any given class to improve and develop the training sessions themselves and an individual's skills as a trainer.

Trainer effectiveness can be evaluated in a number of different ways. These generally break down into three types:

> peer evaluation, in which trainers are evaluated by fellow staff members or trainers

> participant evaluation, in which students evaluate trainers' teaching style and effectiveness

> self-evaluation, in which trainers evaluate their own performance

110

Evaluation can either be formal, as when participants are asked to complete evaluation forms at the close of a training session, or informal, as when trainers circulate among students and ask them their views on the effectiveness of different aspects of a class. You may wish to use more than one type of method to evaluate your trainers and programs.

The following sections outline the different types of evaluation and make recommendations for creating a formal evaluation program and for incorporating evaluators' suggestions during future classes. It is important to take evaluation seriously. Once you have collected feedback on training sessions, act on that feedback. Even if there is no question in your mind or from your institution that patron Internet training is valuable, evaluation offers the opportunity to make training even more valuable for your patrons.

PEER EVALUATION

Trainers who have the opportunity to be observed by other training experts may want to focus their evaluators' attention on areas in which they themselves feel they could use improvement. Trainers might ask peers before a session to pay particular attention to how well they stay on topic, to how clearly they explain Internet terminology, or to whether participants seem unwilling to ask or answer questions. If you as a trainer are going to be observed by a peer, ask for feedback on such specific areas. Take the opportunity to have yourself evaluated by an impartial outside observer, and take the constructive comments to heart.

If you work in a large system with a number of Internet trainers, have the trainers conduct practice training sessions with each other. Practice training can take place during train-the-trainer classes and every once in a while thereafter. Provide the opportunity for trainers to learn from each other and to examine one another's different presentation and teaching styles. Have peer evaluators give their impressions right after the class rather than some time later when their memories have begun to fade.

When asking trainers to evaluate each other, however, emphasize the need for *constructive* criticism. Rather than focusing on describing what another trainer did badly, peers should give suggestions on how to improve, ideas on where a presentation could have been more clear, and so on. You want to avoid a situation in which trainers become jealous or critical of one another; instead, use peer evaluations as a learning situation. Also, give beginning trainers more than one chance to be observed. Give them the opportunity to become accustomed to the observation, and try not to base all comments on one class session that may or may not be typical of their training style.

If you work in a large library district or system and have sufficient staff, you might consider a team-teaching system for your newer trainers. Pairing beginning trainers with more-experienced staff lets beginners observe an expert and gives them the opportunity to be observed and evaluated by more-experienced trainers. Make sure in any team-teaching situation, though, that both trainers have the opportunity to participate. Have trainers introduce one another and alternate teaching sections of the class. Organize materials so that responsibilities are clearly defined, and caution more-experienced trainers to avoid taking over the entire session.

It will be helpful in any team-teaching situation to establish from the beginning that both trainers are partners in facilitating the class. Avoid having the less-experienced person, for example, be the only one to pass out handouts, move chairs around, and dim the lights for a computer presentation. If the newer trainer looks to be the other's gofer, class participants will automatically turn to the trainer who seems to be the class "leader." This will provide little opportunity for the beginning trainer to be observed in a real-life training situation.

PARTICIPANT EVALUATION

Evaluation by participants is the most common type of evaluation and what most trainers may think of when picturing a typical evaluation form or feedback session. When creating participant evaluation forms, be sure to leave room for comments. Trainers who leave space for questions and encourage interaction during training sessions will create an atmosphere in which students will be more willing to take the time to complete evaluations and to provide written comments. This, in turn, leads to more useful information for identifying areas in which your classes need work than just the normal 1-to-5 ranking or yes-or-no questions. Allow participants to complete their forms anonymously so that they are comfortable criticizing either the class or the instructor. You may want to call these sheets "feedback" or "comment forms" to avoid the loaded term "evaluation."

On your feedback forms, ask questions to which you want to know the answers. You'll want to find out whether class objectives were presented clearly, whether your training style was effective and created a comfortable atmosphere, whether handouts and visual aids were sufficient and contributed to participants' understanding of the material, and whether the content met the needs of class participants.

If you are in a large library system with many different trainers, you may want to use the 1-to-5 ranking system on your evaluation forms (while still leaving room for participants to add their own comments). Rankings can then be added and averaged to provide quantitative information about how each trainer is performing in relation to the others.

Keep evaluation forms simple, however. For basic Internet classes, participant evaluation forms should run no longer than one printed page and should take no longer than five or ten minutes to complete. (An example of a typical evaluation form can be found in appendix B.) Remember that adult learners are busy, that their time is valuable, and that you want to make it convenient for them to give their opinions.

While you will probably want to make your evaluation forms somewhat more complex than just asking whether the course was useful or not, remember that the whole thrust of an evaluation is to determine whether the training class had value for the participants and how you could add more value in the future. A good evaluation form will ask for feedback in a variety of areas, including the trainer's effectiveness, the usefulness of class content, and the usefulness of handouts and cheat sheets. It will ask for comments on what was especially helpful during the class as well as what might have been missing.

Try on occasion to create feedback forms that address participants' understanding of each class objective. Ask, for example, whether participants learned in the class how to type in a web address, how to click on a link to go to another web page, how to use the mouse to scroll up and down the page, and how to print out a web page.

For more advanced classes that already have some Internet familiarity, consider providing an online evaluation form and making its completion (near the end of the session) part of the class itself. Present completion of the class evaluation as a useful way of learning to fill out and submit online forms. (See, for example, figure 7.1.) Use any innovative way you can find for getting feedback from participants.

Also make time at the end of any training session to circulate among and talk to the participants. Often, people who will not take the time to fill out an official form will be willing to give you their opinions of the class in person. Take such informal oral evaluations as seriously as you do written evaluation forms; in each case, the person is taking the time to provide you with his or her valuable opinion.

Other forms of informal feedback can be gathered by simply paying attention to participants' reactions during a class. Are they willing to participate? Do they seem enthusiastic? Are they willing to ask and answer questions? Are

FIGURE 7.1
King County (Washington) Library System's Online Evaluation Form

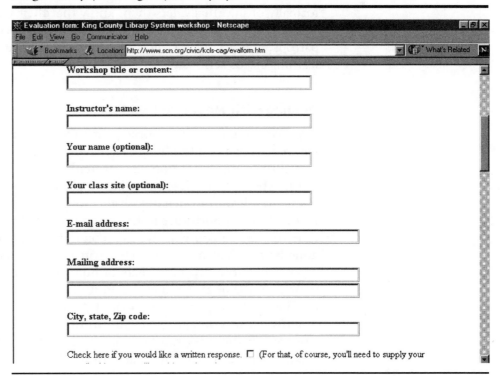

they nodding, grimacing, looking confused? Watching people's responses during a training session provides an instantaneous form of feedback that you can use to modify your behavior during the rest of that class.

Pay attention to whether class participants return to the library to use the Internet after a class session. If you have instilled them with enthusiasm for the medium, they will be likely to come back to try it out on their own. Do they seek you out to ask further questions as their Internet expertise increases? Such unofficial feedback will complement formal evaluation forms and help you see how your classes are meeting participants' needs.

Remember to get feedback and evaluation forms right away. Don't pass out forms to participants as they are leaving and expect them to remember to fill them out and send them back. People's time is valuable, and most just will not bother. Give them out either at the beginning of the class or at the end, but be sure to mention the form. If you are conducting a long session, especially if it is in a private computer lab, consider allowing an extra five or so minutes at the end for participants to complete the forms. Don't just include the evaluation form in a packet of handouts and expect that people will find and complete it; make a point of mentioning the importance of feedback and say that you are looking forward to their suggestions. Ask participants to be honest, and tell them that their forthright comments will help improve the class for others. Thank participants ahead of time for their input.

If you receive very little feedback from learners, or if few people complete evaluation forms, examine how you appear to class participants. Do you appear to welcome feedback? Have you encouraged people to complete their feedback forms? Watch for nonverbal signals you may be sending out; if you truly dread being evaluated, you may inadvertently be sending that message to participants.

Last, understand that eliciting feedback from class participants, whether formally or informally, lets them know that their wants and needs are important to your library. Any training is a two-way process between you and your patrons, and asking for their feedback shows that you take them and their learning needs seriously.

Dealing with Negative Feedback

Yes, every trainer will at some point receive a negative evaluation. Maybe you're having a bad teaching day, maybe there is just no pleasing one of your participants, maybe respondents weren't ready for that particular class. But, just maybe, it is possible that your negative evaluator has some constructive points. Look at most negative evaluations as constructive criticism, providing you with the opportunity to grow as a trainer. If class participants have taken time to provide you with written comments on how the session could have gone better, they are really giving you a gift of their opinions.

We all know two basic facts of human nature: People are more likely to remember the negative than the positive and are more likely to complain than to praise. Participants who would have no qualms about opening their mouths if a session fails to live up to their expectations may leave without a word when the class satisfies their needs. As a trainer, therefore, you will inevitably need to learn to deal with negative feedback.

You can usually easily distinguish between constructive feedback and a cheap shot at you as a trainer because the respondent is disgruntled about something else entirely. Maybe that person had a bad day and is taking it out on you. Try not to take that sort of criticism personally. If you receive one negative evaluation in a stack of positive feedback, you can take it less seriously. However, if a significant percentage of your participants seem to have negative comments, especially if they're all objecting to the same aspect of the class, then study these comments carefully. Look for trends. Your participants are trying to tell you how your program could have been more effective. Remember that the most important rule of training is to approach your classes from the point of view of the participant, teaching them what they need to know. If they are leaving unsatisfied, then you are falling short in your job as a trainer.

Also remember that no one starts out as the "perfect" trainer and that learning from experience is the way we grow. Getting feedback from participants, whether positive or negative, is one avenue for self-improvement.

Match feedback from participants to your own gut feelings about your performance. As an exercise, try completing your own evaluation form. Make note of what you did particularly well during the session, as well as of where you think you could have improved. Now look at the evaluations from class participants. How well do they match your own feelings about the session? Did people comment on the positive as well as the negative aspects of the class?

SELF-EVALUATION

Another important component of the evaluation process is self-evaluation. Consider creating a self-evaluation form for trainers or having them informally assess themselves after training sessions. Trainers can then compare their own impressions of a session with those of the participants.

Remember that here, too, it can be easier to focus on the negative than on the positive. Trainers should make a conscious effort to focus on what they did right during a session as well as on where they might have improved. If you use a self-evaluation form, include questions such as

What did I do right during this session?

What was the best aspect of my presentation?

What objective did I explain particularly well?

Balance these out with questions such as

What mistakes did I make during the session?

Where could my presentation have been more clear?

Self-evaluation questions should be open-ended; compare them with the feedback forms you receive from class participants. See if your own honest impressions of a class match those of the attendees.

Some trainers, especially those in large systems or whose only duty is as a trainer, may want to videotape or audiotape themselves during a session. Keep in mind, however, that the presence of a video camera will be intimidating—

not only to you as a trainer but to your participants as well. Beginners, especially, may be reluctant to participate if they know that they are being recorded. So videotaping, while a useful tool in observing your own teaching style, is a better choice for a practice session than for use during an actual class. Also, never make videotaping mandatory for any trainer. Some people have a viscerally negative reaction to the idea of being captured on tape, and you don't want them to have such negative associations with training itself.

Consider making a preclass checklist of what you want to get across in each session and how you want to improve your presentation. After class, go through your list and identify the areas you need to focus on the next time. Before each session, try to identify at least one or two areas you want to improve, and create a strategy for doing so.

USING EVALUATION TO IMPROVE YOUR TRAINING STYLE

Use evaluations as a tool to improve your own skills as a trainer. A useful exercise is to go over the evaluation forms from your last few Internet training sessions and identify ways in which you are doing well and areas in which participants feel your training could use improvement. Decide on a specific course of action for improving your skills, and focus on continuing the things you are doing right.

Don't be afraid to change. Just because one way of training appears to be working well enough is not an excuse to avoid trying new ideas. Avoid getting locked into always presenting a class in an identical manner, although this is easy enough to do after you have taught a number of sessions on the same topic. Repeating the class the very same way each time will eventually dampen your own enthusiasm for training.

EVALUATING THE PROGRAM ITSELF

Evaluation is important not only for individual trainers but for an institution's program as a whole. After a trainer has had the opportunity to peruse his or her class evaluation forms, copies should be given to the training coordinator, administrator, or other individual responsible for planning the Internet training program.

You will regularly find it necessary to update the content of your Internet training classes as technology changes, new browser versions emerge, web sites go down, and so on. When proceeding with such an update, also go through class evaluations from all of your trainers and see where the content of your training sessions could be improved so that you can provide an even greater value to your patrons.

Recognizing that your training sessions and trainers are continually developing does not mean anything is necessarily "wrong" with the way you have been teaching. The fact that your library teaches Internet classes well does not mean that you cannot teach them better. The best trainers always try to improve their training style and the content of their classes. Avoid becoming too comfortable and allowing trainers to stagnate—they will eventually become bored and will transmit that boredom to participants. Encourage trainers to innovate, and recognize that we are all continually learning. In the same way that reference personnel, for example, develop their skills by attending conferences and workshops, trainers need similar opportunities to grow.

Remember that your trainers are also learners. Provide them with regular opportunities to update their training skills through workshops, newsletters, and other materials. Provide an opportunity for trainers to meet with each other and with the library's administration to discuss how classes are going and to brainstorm ideas on updating and expanding your offerings.

Evaluation is also important to provide ammunition for the continuation of your Internet training program. Both evaluation forms and informal anecdotes can show your administration the value that attending classes has had for your patrons.

Regular evaluation and an honest dialogue with your patrons will help you keep your library's Internet training program helpful and relevant to your community. Through listening to your patrons' needs and always remaining willing to innovate, your institution can create classes that will draw in a variety of customers.

Use the ideas presented in this book in conjunction with those you gain from your fellow librarians and Internet trainers as well as those suggested by your patrons themselves. Whatever the size of your library or the scope of your Internet training program, you will be providing your community with a significant service that will enable users to make better use of online resources both within and outside the library environment.

Recommended Resources for Developing an Internet Training Program

Listed in this section are general books, web sites, electronic discussion lists, and journal articles that should help Internet trainers in any library develop their training programs. Suggestions of materials on more specific subjects (such as teaching Spanish speakers or seniors) can be found in the resources sections of the respective chapters.

GENERAL COMPUTER TRAINING

Although relatively little has been written on the specific aspects of Internet and other public computer training in libraries, general and corporate computer training manuals abound. Following are some of the more useful publications in that area.

Agre, Phil. "How to Help Someone Use a Computer." Adapted and available: http://www.compumentor.org/cm/resources/articles/117.html. First published in *The Network Observer* 1, no. 5 (May 1994).

Commonsense and straightforward advice on helping computer beginners.

Clothier, Paul. *The Complete Computer Trainer.* New York: McGraw-Hill, 1996.

Everything you wanted to know about teaching computer technology. Although examples are dated, principles are still sound.

Elliott, Franki. "Searchers as Teachers and Entertainers." *Searcher: The Magazine* 6, no. 7 (July/Aug. 1998): 28–32.

Describes how to make training effective and interesting.

Kovacs, Diane. *The Internet Trainer's Total Solution Guide*. New York: Van Nostrand Reinhold, 1997.

Although the information here is becoming somewhat dated, the book remains one of the few resources aimed directly at Internet trainers.

Masie, Elliott. *The Computer Training Handbook: Strategies for Helping People to Learn Technology*. Minneapolis: Lakewood Books, 1997.

A thorough introduction to how people learn technology, including many techniques for training others to use computers.

NETTRAIN

Electronic discussion list for computer and Internet trainers. Subscribe by sending an e-mail message to listserv@ubvm.cc.buffalo.edu. In the body of the message, type: subscribe NETTRAIN (insert your first and last name). NETTRAIN is a list every Internet trainer should subscribe to. Participants gladly provide information and examples from their own training experience.

Weiss, Elaine. *The Accidental Trainer: You Know Computers, So They Want You to Teach Everyone Else*. San Francisco: Jossey-Bass, 1997.

A good book for those who are thrust into Internet training responsibilities with little formal preparation.

THE INTERNET IN LIBRARIES

Some useful material is finally beginning to emerge on the specific issue of Internet training in libraries. Following are some suggestions for additional resources that may help in planning your own training program. Although few address only the issue of providing public Internet training, these resources will help get you thinking about not only training but all the other aspects of providing public Internet access in your institution.

American Library Association. *Libraries & the Internet Toolkit: Tips and Guidance for Managing and Communicating about the Internet*. Chicago: American Library Assn., 2000.

Focus is largely on filtering and on serving children in an age of technology. Includes tips on creating a policy, examples of useful Internet programs in many public libraries, and tips on handling questions from patrons and the press.

Benson, Allen. *Complete Internet Companion for Librarians*. New York: Neal-Schuman, 1997.

A thorough discussion of all aspects of the Internet in libraries. Especially helpful for those just bringing Internet to their institution.

————. *Connecting Kids and the Internet: A Handbook for Librarians, Teachers, and Parents.* New York: Neal-Schuman, 1999.

Good information for those planning classes for parents, teachers, or children.

Buildings, Books, and Bytes: Libraries and Communities in the Digital Age. Washington, D.C.: The Benton Foundation, 1996. Available: http://www.benton.org/Library/Kellogg/ buildings.html.

Gives some helpful background on public attitudes toward public libraries and technology. Shows what the public expects from libraries in the Internet age.

Hollands, William. *Teaching the Internet to Library Staff and Users.* New York: Neal-Schuman, 1999.

A series of scripted workshops for library Internet trainers. Must be adapted for particular situations.

Kovacs, Diane, and Michael Kovacs. *The Cybrarian's Guide to Developing Successful Internet Programs and Services.* New York: Neal-Schuman, 1997.

A bit of information about training but focused more on using the Internet in reference, providing library information online, and establishing Internet use in the library.

Martin, Lyn Elizabeth M., ed. *The Challenge of Internet Literacy: The Instruction-Web Convergence.* New York: Haworth, 1997.

An anthology of articles aimed at describing the theory behind providing instruction and getting students to think critically about online resources in academic libraries.

TEACHING THE USE OF ELECTRONIC RESOURCES IN LIBRARIES

Material on teaching the use of electronic resources in libraries, while not specific to Internet training, addresses similar and related issues. Today, many electronic library resources are Internet based and more are moving in that direction. The following books and web sites discuss the introduction and teaching of electronic resources in libraries. Although many of the particular examples are becoming outdated, the general principles remain useful.

Barclay, Donald, ed. *Teaching Electronic Information Literacy: A How-to-Do-It Manual for Librarians.* New York: Neal-Schuman, 1995.

Aimed largely at academic institutions. Addresses teaching electronic resources and when their use is appropriate.

Computers in Libraries 20, no. 3 (March 2000).

> A theme issue with several articles on teaching technology in libraries. Includes articles on computer-based training, teaching hands-on classes to working professionals, and teaching information literacy in a college environment.

LaGuardia, Cheryl, and others. *Teaching the New Library: A How-to-Do-It Manual for Librarians.* New York: Neal-Schuman, 1996.

> Addresses how traditional bibliographic instruction is transformed in a technological era and predicts how libraries' roles will change in the future. Largely focused on academic libraries.

Management Committee of the Machine-Assisted Reference Section, Reference and User Services Association, American Library Association. *Guidelines for the Introduction of Electronic Information Resources to Users.* (Chicago: American Library Assn., 1997). Available: http://www.ala.org/rusa/stnd_electron.html.

> Discusses how to effectively introduce new electronic resources in libraries. Goes through the stages of teaching resources to staff and then to patrons.

PRESENTATION/TRAINING SKILLS

There are a plethora of books and other materials directed toward trainers and presenters. See what is available in your own library, but following are a few suggestions of especially useful materials. These items will assist beginning trainers in honing their presentation and training skills and in planning their training program.

Charles, C. Leslie, and Chris Clarke-Epstein. *The Instant Trainer: Quick Tips on How to Teach Others What You Know.* New York: McGraw-Hill, 1998.

> Useful volume, laid out in a question-and-answer format.

Doylan, Bob. *What's Your Point? A Proven Method for Giving Crystal Clear Presentations.* Wayzata, Minn.: Point Publications, 1988.

> Especially helpful to trainers who will be doing a presentation using PowerPoint or other software as part of their class sessions.

Hendricks, William, and others. *Secrets of Power Presentations.* Franklin Lakes, N.J.: Career, 1996.

> Useful for trainers who need to brush up on their presenting skills.

Klatt, Bruce. *The Ultimate Training Workshop Handbook.* New York: McGraw-Hill, 1999.

> Everything you wanted to know about setting up a training session, from room layouts to theories of adult learning to effective presentation styles.

"TrainingSuperSite." Minneapolis: Lakewood Publications, 1997–2000. Available: http://www.trainingsupersite.com.

Online training resources in a variety of areas, focused largely on technology training. Can subscribe to training magazines and newsletters and participate in online discussions.

Weiss-Morris, Loretta. "Quick Training Tips." Hopatcong, N.J.: Systems Literacy, 1991–2000. Available: http://quicktrainingtips.com.

At the site, visitors can also sign up for the free "Quick Training Tips" electronic newsletter. Short anecdotes, analogies, and examples that will help you become a more effective trainer.

B

Sample Handouts, Forms, and Other Materials

Following are some examples of handouts, worksheets, forms, and other materials that will be useful as you begin planning your Internet training program. Adapt these samples as necessary for your own institution.

Staff Self-Assessment Worksheet for Netscape Communicator

Checklist for Evaluating Internet Information

Evaluation Form for Internet-for-Beginners Classes

Press Release for Free Internet Basics Class

Handout for Internet Basics Class on Netscape Communicator 4.72

Handout for Internet Basics Class on Internet Explorer 5

Printout Directions for Netscape Communicator

Handout on E-Mail and Web Addresses

Résumé Examples for Job Searching on the Internet

Advertisement for an Internet Basics Class

Staff Self-Assessment Worksheet
for Netscape Communicator

Directions: Please rate your skills in the following areas from 1 to 3.

    1 = you have little confidence in your ability in this area

    2 = you are somewhat comfortable with your ability
        to complete the given skill

    3 = you are completely confident in your ability
        to complete the skill

1. I know how to use Netscape to visit a web page whose address I know.

        1   2   3

2. I can recognize and click on links to move to different web sites.

        1   2   3

3. I am comfortable using Netscape bookmarks to organize my favorite web sites into folders and can easily use bookmarks to visit those sites again.

        1   2   3

4. I am familiar with the function of each button on the Netscape toolbar.

        1   2   3

5. When I get a "File Not Found" error I know how to "back up" through a web site address to try and find where the page may have been moved.

        1   2   3

6. I know how to use "Print Preview" to find and print out only part of a long web site.

        1   2   3

7. I am comfortable using Netscape preferences to change web page colors and fonts.

        1   2   3

8. I know how to set the Netscape home page.

        1   2   3

9. I know how to copy and save a web site image onto my own hard drive.

        1   2   3

10. I am comfortable using copy and paste to move text from a web page into my word processor.

        1   2   3

11. I am able to use Netscape's history file to find pages where I have been before.

        1   2   3

12. I can use the drop-down arrow by the location bar to visit recent sites.

        1   2   3

Checklist for Evaluating
Internet Information

1. Do the author's name and credentials appear clearly
   on the page?   _____ Yes   _____ No

2. Is the author an authority on this subject?   _____ Yes   _____ No

3. Does the author have anything to gain by presenting
   this information?   _____ Yes   _____ No

4. Is the information consistent with what you can find
   in other sources?   _____ Yes   _____ No

5. Is the information current and up to date?   _____ Yes   _____ No

Evaluation Form
for Internet-for-Beginners Classes

Date and time of class: _____

Directions: Please circle the appropriate response after each statement.

5 = strongly agree   1 = strongly disagree

1. The information presented in this class will help me use the Internet at the library.

   1   2   3   4   5

2. The handouts were helpful and relevant to the material covered in the class.

   1   2   3   4   5

3. The instructor was knowledgeable about the Internet.

   1   2   3   4   5

4. What would have made this class more useful for you?

5. Additional comments:

Press Release
for Free Internet Basics Class

FOR IMMEDIATE RELEASE [date]

Contact: [Your name and phone number]

[Name of Library] Offers Free Internet Training

The [name of your library] has announced a new program to bring free Internet training workshops to the [name] community.

"We're very excited about this opportunity to help our patrons learn the Internet skills that are becoming more and more essential in the Information Age," says [name of director], director of the [name of library]. "From employment resources to genealogy to electronic mail, our technology trainers can help people learn to find the information they need online."

As an information center, the [name of library] provides much more than books. By providing free Internet access at library terminals, the library enables all members of the community to take advantage of online resources. This new training program will help residents make better use of such resources.

"We want everyone to be able to take advantage of the wonderful technological resources the library provides," says [name of Internet trainer]. "Everyone should feel welcome in our introductory classes, and we provide a way for beginners to get instruction on using the Internet at the library in a comfortable, nonthreatening atmosphere."

– more –

The [name of library] has provided free Internet access to the community since [date]. For more information about the library's Internet training program or to sign up for a free class session, call the library at [phone number].

# # #

Handout for Internet Basics Class
on Netscape Communicator 4.72

Using Netscape Communicator at the Library

 The **Back** button always brings you back exactly one page from where you are on the Internet.

 The **Forward** button will bring you one page forward from where you are. Watch how the Forward button is grayed out and lighter until you use the Back button to move backward.

 You can use the **Reload** button to refresh your view of a web page. For example, on a fast-news day when you are looking at a site such as cnn.com, you can use Reload to see if the site has updated its headlines. Reload will tell the software to go out and get the newest, freshest copy of that web page.

 The **Home** button will bring you back to the page you have set as your home page. On any of the library's Internet computers, the Home button will always take you back to the library's own web site.

 The **Search** button will take you to a web page where you can search for information on the Internet.

 Use the **Print** button to print out a web page.

 The **Security** button's lock will close up and it will turn bright yellow when you are on a web page that has extra security in place. Do not put in personal information such as a credit card number or social security number unless you see that the lock is closed up and yellow.

 Use the **Stop** button to tell the computer to stop trying to load a web page that is loading too slowly or that looks like it's stuck.

Handout for Internet Basics Class
on Internet Explorer 5

Using Internet Explorer at the Library

The **Back** button always brings you back exactly one page from where you are on the Internet. Use the little arrow next to the button to see the last couple of places you have visited.

The **Forward** button will bring you one page forward from where you are. Watch how the Forward button is grayed out and lighter until you use the Back button to move backward.

Use the **Stop** button to tell the computer to stop trying to load a web page that is loading too slowly or that looks like it's stuck.

You can use the **Refresh** button to reload your view of a web page. For example, on a fast-news day when you are looking at a site such as cnn.com, you can use Refresh to see if the site has updated its headlines. Refresh will tell the software to go out and get the newest, freshest copy of that web page.

The **Home** button will bring you back to the page you have set as your home page. On any of the library's Internet computers, the Home button will always take you back to the library's own web site.

The **Search** button will take you to a web page where you can search for information on the Internet.

Use the **Print** button to print out a web page.

Printout Directions
for Netscape Communicator

Printing out a web "page" from the Internet is not the same as copying a page out of a book. Sometimes, what you are looking at on the screen can take five, ten, even fifty pages of paper to print out! To avoid getting caught paying for pages and pages of printouts that you do not need, try the following three methods.

1. Take notes! Pens and scratch cards can be found next to each public Internet terminal.

2. Use **Copy** and **Paste** to copy only selected parts of web pages into a text editor, then print out only those parts. To do this,

   a. hold down the left mouse button and drag the mouse to highlight in blue the part of the web page you want to copy

   b. when the part you want is highlighted, click Edit at the top left of the screen

   c. from the menu that pops up, click Copy; the text you want is now copied

   d. minimize Netscape with the minus sign in the upper right-hand corner

   e. open up WordPad by double-clicking the icon on the desktop

   f. click Edit at the top of the screen

   g. click Paste; the text you want should now be pasted into WordPad

   h. print just that text by clicking on the little picture of the printer in WordPad

3. Use **Print Preview** to select only the page(s) you want to print out of Netscape. Click File at the top left of the screen. Click on Print Preview.

   Netscape will show you exactly what the web site will look like on paper when it is printed out. Down in the bottom left-hand corner of the screen, it will show you what page number you are on and how many pages you will have if it is all printed. Although it looks very small, you can zoom in to be able to read better.

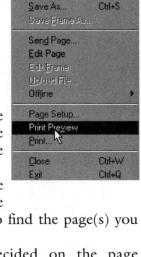

   To zoom in, move your cursor over the page and click once. The page will get bigger.

   Use the Next Page button at the top of the screen to go through to find the page(s) you want to print.

   When you have decided on the page numbers you want, click the Print button at the top of the screen. A printer window will pop up.

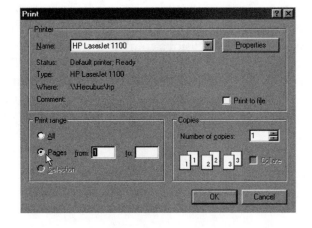

   Click the button next to "Pages," and fill in the exact page numbers you wish to print. Click OK. Netscape will print only those pages. If you want to print only one page, put that page number in both the "from page" and "to page" boxes. (For example, print from page 5 to page 5.)

Handout
on E-Mail and Web Addresses

E-Mail and Web Addresses
How Do I Tell the Difference?

An *e-mail address* allows you to send a personal message to a specific person, much as if you were sending a letter to his or her house. An e-mail address *always* has the @ symbol as part of the address. There are never any blank spaces in an e-mail address.

You can look at an e-mail address to see where the message originated. E-mail is always from a user name at (@) an Internet domain, or particular place on the Internet. The e-mail address identifies the sender of a message just as a return address functions on an envelope. An e-mail address will look like the following:

rachel@lisjobs.com

In the sample e-mail address, "rachel" is a user name that identifies a specific person. A user name is usually selected by that person when he or she signs up for Internet access or for free web-based e-mail. Also, "lisjobs.com" is the Internet domain the person is using to send the message. This is usually the place where the writer gets Internet access or free e-mail. Put an e-mail address such as the one in this example into the "To:" line when you are composing an e-mail message to send that message to a particular person just as you would write an address on an envelope.

A *web site address* (sometimes called a *URL*, for Uniform Resource Locator) allows you to visit a particular *place* on the World Wide Web to view a particular web site. A web site address *never* has an @ symbol as part of the address. There are never any blank spaces in a web site address.

Web site addresses often, but not always, start with the letters "www" (for World Wide Web). A typical web site address will look like the following:

www.lisjobs.com

If you type the above web site address into the address bar of your browser, you will be transported to that particular web site.

Sometimes you will see "http://" (for Hyper-Text Transfer Protocol) printed before a web site address. You do not need to type that part in—the software will figure it out by itself.

Résumé Examples
for Job Searching on the Internet

A. FORMATTED IN MICROSOFT WORD

Jane Smith

Employment: ANYTOWN PUBLIC LIBRARY, Anytown, Ill.
Head, Computer Services Department, June 1999–present

- Created and implemented library's Y2K readiness plan

- Planned, installed, and administered local NT network

- Designed and maintained library's web page:
  http://www.anytownlibrary.org

Reference/Computer Services Librarian, May 1998–May 1999

- Created and maintained both internal web sites and printed handouts to guide users of public-access Internet terminals

- Organized and taught public Internet training classes

- Maintained and organized library computer equipment and software

Reference Librarian, September 1996–April 1998

- Developed and maintained collection of Spanish-language materials for adults

- Created and led bimonthly book discussion groups

(continued)

B. FORMATTED AS TEXT-ONLY FOR E-MAIL OR WEB FORM

Jane Smith

Employment:

ANYTOWN PUBLIC LIBRARY, Anytown, Ill.

Head, Computer Services Department
June 1999-present

* Created and implemented library's Y2K readiness plan
* Planned local NT network
* Developed and maintained library's web page: http://www.anytownlibrary.org

Reference/Computer Services Librarian
May 1998-May 1999

* Created and maintained both internal web sites and printed handouts to
guide users of public-access Internet terminals
* Organized and taught Internet training classes for patrons
* Responsible for maintenance and organization of library computer
equipment and software

Reference Librarian
September 1996-April 1998

* Started and maintained collection of Spanish-language materials for adults
* Created and led bimonthly adult book discussion groups

Advertisement for an Internet Basics Class

Feel Lost Using the Internet? We're Here to Help!

The library is offering free Internet training to beginners.

No previous computer knowledge is assumed.

We will teach you the basics of using a mouse and the

web browser in the library.

Classes last about one hour

and are taught by a member

of our reference department.

Sign up today at the

Front Desk!

Index

Note: Page numbers in **bold face** refer to figures.

Rachel Singer Gordon is head of computer services at the Franklin Park (Illinois) Public Library. She has planned, scheduled, and taught public Internet classes there since 1998. Gordon earned her undergraduate degree at Carleton College. She received her MA in modern Judaism from Northwestern University and her MLIS from Dominican University (formerly Rosary College). Since 1996, she has maintained a web site for job-seeking librarians at http://www.lisjobs.com.

T. W. Phillips Memorial Library
Bethany College
DISCARD